I0426520

SOMEHOW IT WORKS

A Story of U.S. Presidential Elections

By

John L. McCloskey

This book is a work of non-fiction. Names and places have been changed to protect the privacy of all individuals. The events and situations are true.

© 2003 by John L. McCloskey. All rights reserved.

No part of this book may be reproduced, stored in a retrieval system, or transmitted by any means, electronic, mechanical, photocopying, recording, or otherwise, without written permission from the author.

ISBN: 1-4107-6451-6 (e-book)
ISBN: 1-4107-7103-2 (Paperback)

This book is printed on acid free paper.

1stBooks - rev. 07/21/03

DEDICATION

This book is dedicated to Mr. Frank Brown, former history professor at The University of Scranton, PA. A scholar and teacher, Mr. Brown instilled in me and others in his classes a genuine love of history. I credit my interest in U.S. history to the enthusiasm Mr. Brown injected in his classes.

My chief regret is that I never told him what influence he had on my life—but somehow I think he knew.

Also, to my wife, Marie, who kept encouraging me to continue when I felt like putting down the pen, and also for letting me borrow her shoulder when the publishers' rejections flowed in.

iv

INTRODUCTION

"Democracy is the worst form of government in the world except for everything else that's been tried."
Winston Churchill

Every four years in America qualified voters go to the polls to cast their ballot for their favorite candidate for President and Vice President of the United States. They ideally base their decision on the stand the candidates take on the burning issues facing this country. Aware of this, candidates attempt to give something for everyone as they "stump the country" in search of support. The Midwestern and Corn Belt areas and all farmers in general will be promised parity payments for surplus farm products; the National Association of Manufacturers will have nothing to fear from foreign imports, or high excess profits taxes; the industrial workers will be told that collective bargaining will be forever guaranteed; women will achieve their rightful place in the work force with commensurate pay; and equal rights will most certainly be guaranteed for all minorities. In short, every four years emerge vibrant, inexhaustible, almost superhuman individuals who know exactly what is wrong with this country and know precisely what to do to correct the deficiencies.

After all the stumping is over and the various primaries are conducted we then witness the extravaganza which would make Barnum and Bailey very envious. We call it a convention and both Democrats and Republicans have them; this is where the "brass ring" will be for all candidates to grasp. Many Americans will complain bitterly that their favorite television programs are preempted by the networks' convention coverage, but down deep they all love to hear that delegate say, "the great State of Delaware, that small wonder, the state that started a nation, the chemistry capital of the nation and home of the fighting Blue Hens, passes.

Democrats and Republicans will eventually select a candidate to represent them in the general election, and on the first Tuesday following the first Monday in November the people will vote for the candidate of their choice. Newspapers will blare out the results the following day (TV, fifteen minutes after the polls close in the East). In both cases the announcement will be premature. The election results will not be decided until the following month at which time the electors will cast the official ballots.

The U.S. Constitution is very clear on the election of a President of the United States. It states that following the general election in November the electors representing the victorious party in their state will proceed to their state capitol and cast their ballot for a presidential candidate. (Each state will have as many electoral votes as they have Senators and Representatives and all of the electors in all of the states collectively are known as The Electoral College.) When this procedure is concluded in all the states, the votes are sealed and sent to the President of the Senate where, in the presence of both houses of

Congress, the votes shall then be opened and counted. The candidate receiving a simple majority of the votes shall become President. If no candidate receives a majority of the votes cast then the House of Representatives will be called upon to make the decision from among the top three candidates each state will then have but one vote. Once this procedure is concluded the President of the United States is officially elected. At this point it is interesting to point out that only twice in our history of presidential elections did no candidate receive a majority of the electoral votes—1800 and 1824. It is also necessary to point out that electors are not obligated (except by conscience) to vote for the candidate carrying their state except where state law requires that this be done. It has happened very infrequently, but there have been cases where electors voted their own preference rather than the mandate from the states' voters.

One aspect of our political process that has come under criticism for many years is the manner in which the President is elected. The electoral college is the culprit in this case. While a simple majority of the electoral votes is required for a candidate to be elected President, it is interesting to note that a simple majority of the popular vote of the state is all that is required for a candidate to receive all the electoral votes of that state. Consider for a moment that if a candidate receives only one popular vote less than the victorious candidate—*all* the electoral votes of the state will go to the victor. Consider further that a candidate receives all of the popular votes of thirty-nine states and one less than half of the popular votes the victor receives in the eleven highest electoral count states - he will lose the election to his opponent. It becomes apparent then that eleven states can elect the President, and that the overwhelming choice of the people can lose the election. This, I'm sure, helps account for lack of interest in voting on the part of many people.

While the above example of the popular vote landslide of the losing candidate is highly unlikely, our Constitution permits it. It could happen. When we cover the election of 1912 it will be shown that Woodrow Wilson acquired 435 electoral votes, Theodore Roosevelt, 88 and William Howard Taft, 8 electoral votes, and Woodrow Wilson was a minority president receiving less than half of the popular votes. So it could also appear that a candidate won in a landslide when actually it could have been a close race.

It seems to many that the electoral system of electing the President has outlived its usefulness; it has been under attack for years. Some of the critics would have the President elected by popular vote. Others would give the candidate that percentage of the states electoral votes as he had popular votes. There are many, however, who believe it to be almost sacrilegious to change what our founding fathers in all their wisdom created. If only these people would take the time to realize that it was Alexander Hamilton who vehemently fought for the electoral system because he did not want to entrust the average person with such an important decision, then they might be more inclined to seek a better, more equitable method of selecting our chief executive.

The amazing thing about the political process in America is that somehow it works. With all of the hoopla and fanfare preceding the general election and the lack of seriousness many people give to the importance of voting, many outstanding leaders have been turned out who have left an indelible mark in our nation's history.

In the following study of Presidential elections held in the United States it will be noted that those elections of special importance will be treated in detail while the elections of lesser significance will be treated superficially. Events of the various presidential administrations will be limited in treatment to those which in some major way influenced the reelection bid of the incumbent.

SOMEHOW IT WORKS

The first Presidential election held in the United States occurred in the year 1789—thirteen years following its separation from Great Britain. Political parties had not yet emerged in the United States and so we find that our first President, George Washington, was unopposed when selected by the electoral college. Washington remains to this day the only President unanimously selected by this body. Not even James Monroe who ran unopposed in 1820 could duplicate this feat. (One elector refused to make the selection unanimous because he felt that only Washington should be able to boast of that honor.)

During Washington's administrations the United States government was truly launched. Although not specifically mentioned in the Constitution, Washington selected a group of advisors referred to as a cabinet to help him run the affairs of state, treasury, and war; the federal government made provisions for paying the federal and state debts incurred during the Revolutionary War; the Bill of Rights, the first ten amendments to the Constitution, was ratified; a national bank was chartered; and foreign treaties were made by the United States with Great Britain and with Spain.

Following an active two terms as President of the United States, George Washington, who had won the admiration of all Americans for his early efforts and infinite wisdom in launching our new government declined to seek a third term. This decision of

1

Washington was to set a precedent which would endure for one hundred and forty years. (In 1940, Franklin D. Roosevelt was reelected to an unprecedented third term.)

In his farewell address to the nation, President Washington warned Americans of the undesirable consequences of getting involved in foreign entanglements which might jeopardize our independence; of forming political parties which he felt would have a disrupting influence on our country's unity; and urged that every precaution be taken to prevent a breakup of the Union. (It appears that the United States did remarkably well in ignoring all of these cautions.)

Despite President Washington's caution to avoid political parties, it became inevitable that differences of opinion would surface among Americans when such thorny and controversial issues as a national bank, protective tariff, internal improvements at federal government expense and excise taxes would be debated throughout the land.

There were those in the country who believed that our federal government should be strong and that the state governments should be subservient to it. These same people believed that the rich, able and well-born should become the ruling class. As a benefactor of the manufacturing interests in the country they would strongly support high protective tariffs in an effort to keep foreign competition out of the American market. Such groups found their leader in a New Yorker named Alexander Hamilton and called themselves Federalists.

In contrast to the Federalists many Americans still "fired up" over the rule of King George III opposed a strong federal government and favored strong state governments. These same people strongly believed in a government which would look after and tend to the needs of the "common man". They were opposed to any type of tariff on foreign goods which would raise the price of the manufactured goods they had to purchase. While the cities tended to favor the Federalists, the agrarian interests looked more kindly toward this new group which called themselves Democratic-Republicans and were proud to point to Thomas Jefferson as their leader.

The stage was now set for political rivalry which would persist down through the years. The Federalist party of Alexander Hamilton would eventually be absorbed by a new Whig party during the early 1830's. The Whig party would eventually be replaced by the Republican party in 1856 and would continue to the present as the Republican party. The Democratic-Republican (also called the Republican party, but not to be confused with the present day Republican party) changed its name with the emergence of Andrew Jackson in 1828 and has persisted down to the present as the Democratic party.

The first contested election we had in the United States was in 1796. This election produced rather unusual results by presenting a President and Vice President of opposing parties. To understand how this "one time" situation could occur one has to realize that the Constitution at that time provided that the candidate with the greater number of electoral votes, provided it be a majority, should become president and the candidate with the second greatest number would become Vice President. It so happened that Federalist John Adams received the greatest number of votes and thus became President while Thomas Jefferson, representing the Democratic-Republican party, received the second greatest number of votes and thus became Vice President. It was expected of the electors that they would cast their ballot for the candidate representing their party, but there were some Federalist electors who did not care for Adams and attempted to have Thomas Pinckney, Adams' running mate elected President with Adams as his Vice President. Their little scheme, however, went awry and the awkward consequences previously mentioned resulted. Fortunately for the nation Adams and Jefferson were quite compatible. Following this election it became part of the "unwritten constitution" that electors would cast their ballot for the candidate of the party that they represented. We will find, however, in examining other elections that this practice has not always been followed.

During the administration of John Adams, a rather unhappy administration, problems developed between the United States and France. The XYZ Affair had proved humiliating to the United States and criticism of the Adams administration was mounting. The Federalists, with an eye to the upcoming election of 1800 and a reelection bid resorted to legislation designed to stifle criticism of their party. They passed a series of measures known as the Naturalization, Alien, and Sedition acts. The Sedition Act was the most objectionable since it provided fines and/or imprisonment for anyone found guilty of writing or talking disparagingly about the United States government. Clearly, this was in violation of the United States Constitution's guarantee of freedom of the press and freedom of speech. It would be the undoing of the Federalist party; they were never to elect another President of the United States, and were to disappear completely following the election of 1816.

The Democratic-Republicans had every reason to feel confident of winning the election of 1800. They once again chose Thomas Jefferson to represent them as their presidential candidate and selected Aaron Burr as their Vice Presidential candidate. The Federalists chose the incumbent, John Adams, as their standard bearer. The Democratic-Republicans took full advantage of the unconstitutional laws passed by the Federalists in their attack on John Adams. Personal attacks on Jefferson by the Federalists proved to be of little value. When the electors cast their ballots a very unusual result occurred—Jefferson and Burr were tied for the presidency with seventy-three electoral votes each. It is not altogether surprising that this result occurred since the unwritten constitution (understood as a result of the election of 1796) provided that electors vote only for the candidate of the party they represent.

Since the Constitution mandated that the candidate receiving the greatest number of votes become President Burr felt as eligible for the Presidency as Jefferson even though he knew he was intended for the office of the Vice Presidency only.

The unusual result of this election, however, was not without a prearranged solution. As mentioned earlier, the Constitution provides that the House of Representatives will decide the outcome of any election in which no candidate receives a majority of the electoral votes. When this election went to the House for a solution, the members voted thirty-five times and still came up with a tie vote. The election was finally decided on the thirty-sixth ballot due to the last minute support of Alexander Hamilton who urged Federalist members of the House to vote for Jefferson for President. The outcome was now as most people felt it should be: Jefferson, President - Burr, Vice President. Hamilton's interference with the outcome of this election illustrated that Hamilton's opposition to Jefferson's philosophy of government was dwarfed by Hamilton's distrust and lack of respect for fellow New Yorker, Burr. To prevent such a situation from ever occurring again, the twelfth amendment was added to the Constitution requiring electors to vote on separate ballots their choices for President and Vice President.

In the election of 1804, the Democratic-Republicans again chose Thomas Jefferson to represent them. George Clinton of New York was to be his running mate. The Federalist party selected Charles C. Pinckney and sat back hoping for a miracle. The Democratic-Republicans were extremely confident of winning the election and the results confirmed that their opposition, the Federalists, were a dying breed; the Democratic-Republicans carried all but two states. (Aaron Burr switched to the Federalist party and in this election year ran for Governor of New York. Any chance he had of winning this gubernatorial post was dashed when Alexander Hamilton threw all of his support to Burr's opponent. Burr lost the election and when Burr's demand that Hamilton apologize for remarks he made about Burr during the campaign were refused, Burr challenged Hamilton to a duel, which resulted in the death of Hamilton.)

During Jefferson's administrations the size of the United States nearly doubled with the purchase of Louisiana from France for the paltry sum of fifteen million dollars or a few cents an acre. (Paradoxically, this purchase was opposed by Hamilton who now assumed the posture of a strict interpreter of the U.S. Constitution. He argued that the U.S. Constitution made no mention of granting the Federal government the authority to purchase the territory.) In foreign affairs, the United States won prestige by putting an end to the pirating of ships of Christian nations by the Barbary states of Tripoli, Tunis, Algiers, and Morocco when Stephen Decatur sailed into the Mediterranean with a fleet of ships. His feat was to end the practice of paying ransom to these nations for the return of the ships. Following the precedent set by George Washington, Jefferson chose not to seek a third term in 1808, opening the door for James Madison, the "Father of the Constitution", to become the candidate of the Democratic-Republican party. Madison was opposed by perennial candidate, Charles C. Pinckney, who had run against Jefferson in 1800 and again in 1804. Madison had little difficulty defeating Pinckney and so the chastising of the Federalists continued. Madison was reelected in 1812 defeating Federalist DeWitt Clinton.

The election of 1812 would be our first wartime election. In this election the Federalists enlisted the support of anti-war Democratic-Republicans and almost pulled off a major upset. New England hurt economically by loss of its trade with Great Britain vehemently opposed the war and enthusiastically lent its support to the defeat of Madison.

Following this election DeWitt Clinton could have faded into obscurity but this was not to be - a canal had to be built so that New Yorkers could later make their state the "Empire State". It was the Erie Canal linking New York harbor with Lake Erie. As Governor of New York, Clinton gave tireless effort to the development of "Clinton's Big Ditch" as it was called. Upon completion, New Yorkers experienced a new era of economic growth.

During James Madison's administrations the United States fought a war with Great Britain, the war of 1812, which Madison's adversaries were quick to label, "Mr. Madison's War". The results of the war were indecisive, neither the United States nor Great Britain could claim a clear victory, but the United States stood up to powerful Great Britain once again and this had to count for something for this infant nation.

The Democratic-Republicans in 1816 wanted to see a continuation of the Virginia dynasty (Washington, Jefferson, Madison) as they nominated James Monroe for the Presidency. The terminally ill Federalists would make their last stand in this election;

they would disappear from the political scene nationally. Rufus King was selected by the Federalists and as expected was soundly defeated, but to this day he holds the dubious honor of being the last Federalist candidate for President of the United States. It would be quite inaccurate and rather simplistic to credit the unconstitutional Alien and Sedition acts solely for the demise of the Federalist party from the political scene. For one thing it is felt that the Federalists dragged feet on the nationalistic spirit permeating the country; their opposition to the War of 1812 was felt to be unconscionable by most "star spangled banner" Americans.

James Monroe ran unopposed in the election of 1820. No new party had emerged to replace the deceased Federalists. An accurate assessment of the Monroe period perhaps came from the *Boston Centinel* when they referred to the Monroe years, 1817-1825, as the "Era of Good Feeling". As mentioned earlier, James Monroe received all but one of the electoral votes cast.

Highlighting the Monroe period would be the action that he took to keep foreign powers from exerting economic and political influence over the western hemispheric countries when he proclaimed the Monroe Doctrine in 1823. It was with the knowledge that the British fleet stood ready to aid the United States that our young nation had the audacity to warn powerful European countries to stay out of the western hemisphere.

On the domestic scene the United States was feverishly attempting to carry out a neat balancing act of slave and free states. This problem of slave vs. free states came to the fore when Missouri, a slave state petitioned Congress to enter the Union. If admitted, this would upset the balance of eleven free and eleven slave states being held at this time. Henry Clay, who was eventually to earn the reputation as the "Great Compromiser", settled the issue with what became known as the Missouri Compromise, 1820. Maine, a free territory would enter the Union as a free state and Missouri would enter as a slave state. At best, the Missouri Compromise postponed the inevitable for a period of forty-one years.

The election of 1824 has to be remembered as one of our most important Presidential elections. Sectional interests of the country were paramount during this period. Each section of the country wanted to place a man in the White House to insure that their sectional interests would be propagated. The North would be interested basically in the manufacturing and shipping industries, the South wanted the cotton kingdom perpetuated with, of course, slavery. The West was interested in cheap land and better transportation to get the people out there. To represent the North, John Quincy Adams, son of our second President, was nominated. He came from aristocratic Boston and would add some "dignity" to the campaign. The South nominated William Crawford of Georgia. His health was failing and before the final vote was taken he would suffer a paralytic stroke. The West selected the Battle of New Orleans hero of the War of 1812, Andrew Jackson. A new type of democracy made its appearance with "Andy". It was Jacksonian democracy, the common man advocate. Rounding out the major candidates in this election was the "Great Compromiser", Henry Clay. He called his program the "American System" which put together a program for everyone.

When the votes were tallied it revealed that Andrew Jackson had ninety-nine electoral votes, J.Q. Adams had eighty-four, William Crawford had forty-one and Henry Clay had thirty-seven. In the popular vote column Jackson had almost as many votes as his next two rivals combined. Clearly, no candidate had a majority of the electoral votes and so once again the House of Representatives would be called upon to decide the outcome. Since only the top three candidates would be in contention, Clay was automatically eliminated. Crawford's stroke rendered him unavailable and so the election was really between Adams and Jackson. John Quincy Adams was selected by the House to become our sixth President of the United States and the Jackson camp was fuming. "The will of the people has not been carried out", cried the Jacksonians, but the events that followed have caused historians to ponder this election for many years. It seems that Henry Clay who held the enviable position of Speaker of the House used his influence in the House to get Adams elected over Jackson and shortly following the election Adams named Clay his Secretary of State. "Corrupt Bargain" cries could be heard throughout the United States. It certainly did seem that a deal had been struck up between Adams and Clay. In the Democrats' eyes it was a certainty. There are those who have studied this election and that period of time who are not convinced at all that there was anything suspicious in this election; they argue that Henry Clay was the outstanding American of the time and was the best possible selection that Adams could have made—who knows! So bitter was Andrew Jackson over the outcome of this election that he resigned from the Senate to start campaigning for the election of 1828.

With the demise of the Federalist party following the election of 1816, we witnessed a split in the Democratic-Republican party. In 1824, the faction supporting Adams and his nationalism called themselves National Republicans while the supporters of Andrew Jackson now called themselves Democrats. The Democratic party of Jackson has persisted to the present day under that banner. Fund raising dinners of the Democratic party of today are often referred to as "Jefferson-Jackson Day" dinners.

In 1828, "Old Hickory", as Jackson came to be called entered the fray confident of victory. He would be opposed by the incumbent John Quincy Adams. The campaign turned out to be an attack on the personality of Andrew Jackson, although it is believed that Adams stayed clear of any mudslinging. Jackson had been responsible in his earlier years of having killed several people in duels and his adversaries wanted to make sure that all America heard of this achievement. Undoubtedly, the most scandalous charge leveled against Jackson was really directed toward his wife, Rachel, who was referred to as an adulteress. This charge stemmed from the fact that when Jackson married Rachel she was still legally married. She thought that her divorce from a previous marriage had been finalized. Although they quickly solved this dilemma with a second marriage the damage had been done. Rachel was devastated by the charge. She lived long enough to see her husband elected President of the United States, but not long enough to become the first lady of the land. Her cause of death, according to many was from a broken heart. Jackson reportedly never forgot a friend or forgave an enemy. He would not forget or forgive those responsible for the attack on the woman he loved.

The election of Andrew Jackson to the Presidency in 1828 brought to Washington a new breed of Presidential supporters to witness the inauguration of their hero. They were westerners, the common man, who felt quite responsible for his victory. The residents of Washington, D.C. who had witnessed inauguration ceremonies the likes of those honoring the "Virginia Dynasty" or the Boston Adams' were aghast at the sight of the westerners with their muddy boots climbing atop the upholstered furniture of the White House to catch a glimpse of their product. Trays were knocked over, glass broken, and the President himself escaped bodily harm from well-wishers who wanted to give their "Andy" a good bear hug by being rushed out a side door to safety. One certain outcome of this election which neither political party dared to ignore was that the West served notice that henceforth they were to be a force reckoned with in politics.

One characteristic of the Jackson Presidency was the manner in which he chose those who would be appointed to public office. It was known as the "spoils system" and while Jackson did not invent the spoils system he popularized it by removing hundreds from their posts and replacing them with those who had supported him in his election bid. Jackson felt that this procedure did not measurably affect good government since he firmly believed that one did not have to possess any special talents to hold down a government job and therefore as many people as possible should have the opportunity to serve. Another characteristic of this administration was that of Jackson surrounding himself with "unofficial advisors", mostly newspaper editors, to advise him from time to time on important matters. This group came to be known as "Jackson's Kitchen Cabinet" because it was said that they met in the kitchen and left by the back door. Jackson, however, like his predecessors, did have an official cabinet.

Jackson faced two major problems as he entered the White House. One was the tariff issue which more or less came to a head during his Presidency. The South which always opposed high protective tariffs because it raised the price of manufactured goods they were forced to purchase became incensed when the high tariff of 1832 was levied. (A previous tariff passed in 1828 had been referred to in the South as the "Tariff of Abomination".) South Carolina, so bitterly opposed to this newest tariff, threatened to secede from the Union. Jackson had his own inimitable plan for handling South Carolina and their threat of violence if any attempt was made to collect the tariff in their state but the catastrophic consequences of Jackson's plan was averted when Henry Clay (The Great

Compromiser) recommended a compromise tariff somewhat acceptable to the South.

The other major issue facing Jackson was the issue of rechartering the national bank. The bank charter, a twenty year charter, would expire in 1836. The supporters of the bank aware of Jackson's hatred for the bank and mindful that the President would be seeking reelection in 1832 contrived to bring the issue of the bank charter renewal up four years early to coincide with Jackson's reelection bid. Their rationale was that if Jackson vetoed the bank rechartering it would result in his defeat for reelection. If Jackson accepted the bank charter, the bank would be secure for another twenty years. They were to be wrong on both counts: Jackson put a stinging veto on the bank bill (no surprise at all to those who really knew Jackson) and was reelected to a second term.

The reelection of Jackson in 1832 convinced the President that his veto of the bank bill was favorably received by the people. He therefore embarked on a strategy which would bring on the premature death of the bank; he withdrew federal funds from the national bank and redeposited them in privately owned state banks which had supported him during the election. These banks were quickly dubbed "Jackson's Pet Banks". The "pet banks" engaged in reckless speculation practices by granting loans without adequate collateral and almost completely alienated themselves from acceptable banking principles.

Conscious of the inflated currency now being circulated, the President signed the Specie Circular which required that the sale of public land be paid for in gold or silver. It was inevitable that economic disaster was sure to follow. Since the federal government would not accept the paper currency being circulated by the state banks, the people decided to turn in their paper money for specie with obvious consequences. Banks were unable to provide the specie being demanded and were being forced to close their doors. It came to be known as the Panic of 1837 and was dumped into the lap of Jackson's hand-picked successor, Martin Van Buren.

In 1836 we witness a new political party making its first appearance in a Presidential election. They called themselves Whigs after the British party which opposed the policy of the King. In America it was King Andrew I that they vented all their anger toward. Formed in 1834, the Whigs were a conglomeration of discontents with the Democratic Party and quite eager to reap the spoils of victory. Henry Clay, the acknowledged leader of the Whigs sensing that victory was not in the cards bowed out to William Henry Harrison who had gained fame in the famous battle of Tippecanoe by punishing the raiding Indians just prior to the War of 1812. The strategy of the Whigs in this election was to put four candidates on the ballot to oppose Democrat Martin Van Buren and hopefully prevent any candidate from getting the necessary majority of the electoral votes. They obviously felt that their chances of winning were better with the House of Representatives—they were wrong. Van Buren received more popular votes and more electoral votes than all four Whig candidates combined. Most of the President's attention while in office was devoted to wrestling with the economic disaster presented to him by his predecessor.

"Van, Van, is a used up man" shouted the Whigs enthusiastically as they strutted down the country's main streets in the typical torchlight parades characteristic of that era. The election of 1840 was at hand and the Whigs smelled victory in the air. They had every right to feel confident, the Democrats had lost a lot of friends as a result of the economic times. The Whigs once again turned to William Henry Harrison to represent them and selected John Tyler, a Virginia Democrat, to share the ticket. "Tippecanoe and Tyler Too" was a very catchy slogan and the Whigs used it to their advantage in this campaign.

The Democrats really had no choice but to renominate Martin Van Buren; to do anything else would almost be a clear admission that he was responsible for the economic crisis facing the nation. Of course the Democrats pointed out that the panic in no way could be associated with any policy inaugurated by the Democratic party. Deep down, however, they knew that the odds against them were almost insurmountable. In an attempt to demean Harrison and knock him from the pedestal upon which he was now standing, the Democrats found it necessary to inform the public that the Whig candidate was content to live in a log cabin and drink hard cider all day. This charge proved very damaging to the Democrats when the Whigs forgetting temporarily that Harrison was living in a sixteen room mansion broadcast that their candidate did indeed live in a log cabin and did drink hard cider (the Westerner's drink).

Throughout the country the Whigs threw up hastily constructed log cabins which they used for their headquarters and dispensed hard cider to people as they passed by. This election is often referred to as the "Log Cabin, Hard Cider Campaign".

The popular vote in the election of 1840 was rather close but the Whigs received an overwhelming electoral majority. This election is remembered as a "hollow victory" for the Whigs because Harrison died one month following his inauguration and John Tyler, the Virginia Democrat, assumed the Presidency. It seems that Harrison delivered a lengthy inaugural speech in the rain and hatless, contracted pneumonia and died within one month. It would be misleading, however, to expect that Tyler was a Jackson Democrat; he was anything but that, but he wasn't the Whig President the electorate had voted in in 1840. William Henry Harrison was to become the first President to die while in office and it might be quite logical to surmise that the Whigs probably never even considered that he would not survive his first administration. Instead, they were probably anticipating a fine administration from him and a successful reelection bid.

With the election of 1844 approaching both the Democrats and Whigs started a talent search for a winning candidate. John Tyler's views on government did not measure up to the standards of the Whigs' patriarchs, Daniel Webster and Henry Clay and so was not considered for contention. The Whigs' selection was simplified by the presence of Henry Clay, one of the most popular men in the country at the time. The

Democrats, on the other hand, did not quite have it as easy. There was truly no outstanding Democrat available; they had to decide on James K. Polk, remembered by some as a former Speaker of the House of Representatives and also as governor of Tennessee.

Manifest Destiny, the feeling that the United States should control all area from the Atlantic to the Pacific oceans, was a strong feeling shared by most Americans as the election approached. Specifically, all eyes were focused on Texas; there was a strong desire to make Texas part of the United States. Texas was known as the Lone Star State since declaring her independence from Mexico in 1836. There was also a strong feeling that the northwest boundary of the United States be settled at 54° 40' to settle a boundary dispute between Great Britain and the United States.

The Whigs took the damaging middle of the road on expansionism. The Democrats boldly attacked the issues with the slogans "Reannexation of Texas", (Texas had not been previously annexed), and 54° 40' or Fight", referring to the Oregon Country. The election results sent Clay down to defeat for the third time in his bid for the Presidency. James K. Polk, Democrat, was to win the election without too much room for maneuvering but he wasn't to win 54° 40' he settled for the 49th latitude with Great Britain without a fight. Texas was annexed to the United States in 1845, but the expansionists longed for still more; they looked to the Southwest and to California.

It was during the administration of James K. Polk that the United States became embroiled in a war with Mexico. The Mexican War commenced in 1846 and ended in 1848. The expansionist mood was such during this period that a war with Mexico to grasp control of the Southwest seemed inescapable. Mexico had never recognized the independence of Texas and when the United States annexed Texas in 1845, it was considered unconscionable by Mexico. A boundary dispute developed over the western boundary of Texas. The Mexicans maintained that the boundary was located at the Nueces River while the United States argued that it was farther west at the Rio Grande. A war with Mexico would acquire the vast southwest for the United States so it seemed advisable to the President to dispatch American troops to the disputed Rio Grande area. The Mexicans responded with arms to this "transgression" and thus gave to President Polk the opportunity he so very impatiently awaited.

The President immediately summoned Congress and asked for a declaration of war against Mexico arguing that American blood had been shed on American soil. A member of Congress, Abraham Lincoln, raised the famous Spot Resolutions in which he questioned whether American blood was shed on American soil—if the Mexicans were correct about the western boundary of Texas, American blood was shed on Mexican soil.

The United States defeated the Mexicans in 1848 and as a result partially satisfied the insatiable appetites of the expansionists by acquiring the Southwest for the United States.

The Mexican War was still fresh in the minds of the Americans when the election of 1848 approached. The newly acquired Southwest provided conditions conducive for cotton growing and slavery. Both parties, however, aware that their constituents were found in both the North and the South straddled the slavery issue.

Because President Polk had become ill and was unable to take to the campaign trail the Democrats turned to Lewis Cass who with Stephen A. Douglas had championed the cause of popular sovereignty. The Whigs, on the other hand found a willing candidate in the hero of Buena Vista during the Mexican War, Zachary Taylor—"Old Rough and Ready".

The anti-slavery forces were not at all content to have to choose between the major party candidates and their silence on the slavery issue so they organized their own party, the Free Soil party. Sporting the slogan "Free soil, free speech, free labor and free men", they reactivated a former President, Martin Van Buren. The Free Soil party was adamant that slavery should not be permitted in the territories.

The Free Soilers were able to capture the votes of politically potent New York and with the votes of other Democrats who otherwise would probably have voted for Cass, threw the election to the Whig candidate Zachary Taylor.

The role of third party candidates in American politics has been an interesting one. A characteristic of these "mavericks" is that they tackle issues that the major parties are unwilling to address. It is well documented that when a third party takes a stand on a controversial issue and scores well at the ballot box, one or both of the major parties incorporates that plank in their platform in the following election. Major parties are quite content to let third parties "test the waters". In short, the epitaph of third parties in the United States is that major parties steal their attractive planks.

In 1849 Congress was faced with red hot issues: California was seeking admission to the Union as a free state. At the time there were fifteen free states and fifteen slave states. California's admission would upset the balance in favor of the North. Other thorny issues involved the status of slavery in land recently acquired from Mexico; slavery in Washington, D.C.; a new fugitive slave law, and a boundary dispute between New Mexico and Texas. These issues appeared to be irreconcilable until the "Great Compromiser" Henry Clay came up with his last great compromise - The Compromise of 1850. It was during these crises that friends of Clay cautioned him against suggesting the compromise lest it would jeopardize any future plans he might have for the Presidency. Clay's oft quoted response, "I would rather be right than be President".

The debate raged between the North and South over the compromise. John C. Calhoun, the champion of the South, too ill to walk into the Senate was carried by supporters who read his speech against its ratification. He died before the final vote. The compromise was finally ratified by the necessary two thirds of the Senate but the President did not live to see its passage either. He succumbed in 1850, and was succeeded by his Vice President Millard Fillmore. It seemed that a Whig President could not outlive the high office to which he was elected.

Franklin who? This was a question often heard in the United States following the Democratic convention which met in Baltimore, Maryland, in 1852. Franklin Pierce became the second "dark horse" candidate in our history. Unable to agree on a candidate the Democrats selected this New Hampshire lawyer who had served without distinction as a general during the Mexican War. The one thing in his favor was that he was a pro-slavery Democrat who could be counted on to carry the southern Democrats during the election. His support of the Fugitive Slave Law was particularly appealing to the Southerners. The Whigs were eager to point out that the only battle the general lost was with the bottle.

The Whigs had some outstanding candidates to choose from for this election of 1852. There were no better candidates around than Daniel Webster or Henry Clay, but with the Mexican War and all of its spoils still fresh in the minds of Americans the Whigs chose General Winfield Scott who had served with great distinction during the war. General Scott would have a very difficult time in a Mr. Congeniality contest and this would have to play some role in the outcome of this election. The Whigs, nevertheless, had selected the most durable of all its potential candidates since both Clay and Webster died during the campaign. The Whigs said as little as possible about slavery and they, too, endorsed the Compromise of 1850.

The result of the election while relatively close in the popular vote proved to be a landslide for Franklin Pierce. There was a split in the Whig party between the Northern and Southern factions and this was to prove disastrous for them. This split was to spell the death knoll of the Whig party. They were swallowed up by the new Republican party a few years later.

A new issue appeared on the horizon prior to the election of 1856 which both parties would have been delighted to ignore, but this was not to be; the people demanded to know where each party stood on the issue. The rascal was the Kansas-Nebraska Act, passed in 1854, which stated that the people of these areas should be able to exercise popular sovereignty and decide for themselves the status of slavery in their borders. This act had the effect of rendering the Missouri Compromise inoperable. It was this issue that gave rise to the new Republican party.

The Democrats meeting in convention chose not to stay married to President Pierce; they threw their weight toward James Buchanan, a Pennsylvania lawyer. The Democrats supported the newly passed Kansas-Nebraska Act.

The Republican Party chose John C. Fremont, a noted explorer, as their candidate and opposed the Kansas-Nebraska Act by deploring any further extension of slavery. A popular cry of the Republicans was, "Free soil, free speech, free men, and Fremont". The dying Whigs were able to gasp out a feeble...Fillmore.

The result of the election showed that the Republican party was a force to be concerned about but not strong enough to win the election. James Buchanon was to win the election and to this date holds the distinction of being the only President elected from the historically rich Commonwealth of

Pennsylvania. He also is the only bachelor elected to the White House.

The election further showed that the parties were definitely split along sectional lines. The slavery issue was taking preference over party loyalty. The Northern Republicans were finding an ally in the Northern Democrats and the Southern Democrats found that they had a lot in common with the Southern Republicans. It was also during this period that the South was to earn the title "Solid South" indicating a solid vote for the Democratic party candidates.

In 1858 there was a Senate race in Illinois. Opposing each other for the Senate seat were Stephen A. Douglas, Democrat, and Abraham Lincoln, Republican. While both of these candidates longed for the Senate seat both were painfully aware of the upcoming Presidential election of 1860. This Senate race was highlighted by a series of debates between the two in several towns of Illinois. It was during the debate in Freeport when Lincoln posed a question to Douglas that put "the Little Giant" in a very tight spot. Douglas had been co-author of the Kansas-Nebraska Act, 1854. In 1857, however, the Supreme Court of the United States rendered a decision in the famous Dred Scott case which prohibited the exclusion of slavery anywhere in the United States. Obviously aware that this decision declared the Missouri Compromise unconstitutional and nullified the Kansas-Nebraska Act Lincoln put this question before Douglas: How can you justify your popular sovereignty theory in light of the recent Dred Scott decision?

It's obvious that Lincoln was thinking ahead to the Presidential race of 1860. He knew that Douglas would hurt himself in Illinois and throughout the North if he supported the Dred Scott decision. If he insisted that people should be allowed to decide for themselves regarding slavery then his Presidential hopes for 1860 would be shattered. Douglas thought for what seemed like an hour and came forth with this reply which has come to be remembered as the Freeport Doctrine. Douglas said that a state could refuse to enact legislation supporting slavery and in the absence of such a law slavery could not survive. His answer obviously satisfied the home folk; he won the Senatorial seat. He wasn't so fortunate in 1860.

The slavery issue had been sidestepped rather nicely by the major parties for many years but this was not to be in the 1860 election. Each party knew that the voters wanted to know precisely where they stood on the slavery issue. In this election the Democrats were represented by two candidates, a Northern Democrat and a Southern Democrat. Stephen A. Douglas was selected as the candidate of the Northern Democrats and was ever faithful to his popular sovereignty philosophy in deciding the status of slavery in the territories. The candidate of the Southern Democrats was John C. Breckinridge of Kentucky and called for federal protection of slavery in the territories. A new party, the Constitutional Union party selected John Bell of Tennessee; they wanted to see the Union preserved and the Constitution upheld. The Republican party selected Abraham Lincoln of Illinois who ran on the platform calling for no extension of slavery to the territories.

In analyzing these planks of the various parties dealing with the issue of slavery considering the decision of the U.S. Supreme Court in the recent Dred Scott decision, it appears that Douglas' popular sovereignty would have to be an unconstitutional plank since it offers a method to keep slavery out of the territories; the Republican Party plank on the slavery issue likewise runs counter to the law of the land by limiting slavery to its present boundaries. It would seem that the only legal plank dealing with the slavery issue would be that of the Southern Democrats which called for federal protection of slavery since the Dred Scott decision provided that slavery could exist anywhere in the United States.

A huge dark cloud hovered over this Presidential election. The South had threatened to secede from the Union if Lincoln was elected. Douglas had spread this fear, however ineffectively, during the campaign by maintaining a vote for Lincoln would be a vote for the dissolution of the Union.

The outcome of the election was a great triumph for the "rail splitter". He gathered 180 electoral votes against 123 for all of his opponents combined. In the popular vote, however, Lincoln was to become a minority President. Shortly following the election of Lincoln, the South Carolina legislature seceded from the Union and was quickly followed by six other Southern states. These states early in 1861 met in Montgomery, Alabama, and drafted a constitution for the Confederate States of America.

Fort Sumter, a United States fort located in South Carolina, was running dangerously short of supplies. Lincoln was painfully aware of the possible consequences of supplying the fort for fear it would be interpreted by the Confederacy as an attempt to reinforce the fort. Supply ships were dispatched to the fort which resulted in Fort Sumter being fired upon by the Confederacy. The War Between the States had started and for the next four years the United States would be engulfed in the bloodiest war of its history with brother fighting against brother and fathers fighting against sons.

Lincoln's inaugural address was both conciliatory and firm. While he chided the Confederate states for secession he was quick to point out that there was no provision in the Constitution for such an act. He pointed out that there would be no conflict unless they (The Confederacy) became the aggressor.

Meanwhile there were eight slave states debating the merits of following her seven sister states. Arkansas, Tennessee, North Carolina and Virginia did finally decide to join the Confederacy. The loss of Virginia to the Union was a stunning blow. For one thing it placed the Confederacy at the back door of the Nation's capital and secondly it meant that the Union lost the ablest of generals that the War Between the States produced, Robert E. Lee. A West Pointer, Lee did not find his decision easy to make; in the final analysis Lee chose to decline Lincoln's offer to lead the Union troops. "How can I draw my sword against my native Virginia," Lee proclaimed. The border slave states that decided to remain in the Union were

Delaware, Kentucky, Maryland, and Missouri. It took a bit of persuasion to get Kentucky and Missouri to stay "pat".

President Lincoln's administration was plagued with problems at home as well as in the South. For one thing his cabinet was not renowned for its loyalty and secondly numbered among members of Congress were a group known as the Copperheads who opposed the war and worked toward discouraging enlistments and encouraging desertions.

The Confederacy had put a lot of faith in acquiring support from Great Britain. They felt that "cotton is king" and the textile mills of Britain would so sorely need this export that they would actively come to the aid of the South. Great Britain did send money, supplies, and warships to aid the Confederate cause but the aid stopped short of actual military support. Sympathy for the Confederacy did run high in Great Britain; they looked upon the plight of the South as that of gaining independence. Aware of this, Lincoln wanted as succinctly as possible to make the British aware that the war was being fought over slavery, not over any compelling desire for independence on the part of the South. (Britain had already prohibited slavery at home.) The manner in which Lincoln promulgated this information to the British was through the Emancipation Proclamation in which he proclaimed that all slaves residing in the states which were in rebellion against the United States were thenceforth and forever set free.

In 1863 following the bloodiest three day battle of the war, President Lincoln traveled to a small

Pennsylvania town, Gettysburg, to deliver a message honoring those who had given their lives and to pledge that they had not died in vain.

General George B. McClellan of the Union army was not living up to the expectations of Lincoln. At one point during the war Lincoln made the statement, "McClellan's got the slows." At another point during the war Lincoln was very annoyed that McClellan always overestimated the enemy and underestimated his own strength and was reported to have sent the message to McClellan that if he wasn't going to use the army he would like to borrow it because there was a war in progress. All of this criticism of McClellan and McClellan's dissatisfaction with the leadership that Lincoln was providing during the war decided to enter the political arena in 1864 and run for the Presidency on the Democratic ticket.

In an effort to win the support of the northern Democrats in the election of 1864 the Republicans changed their name and now called themselves the Union Party. They placed Andrew Johnson from Tennessee and a former slaveholder on the Union ticket as Lincoln's running mate in order to win the vote of the border states.

As election day approached it did not look as though the President would be reelected to a second term; the conduct of the war was going against the Union. There were many supporters of Lincoln in the election of 1860 who began to have second thoughts about his leadership Maybe McClellan is right, they began to reason.

Fortunately for the Union party William Tecumseh Sherman was making his famous march to divide the Confederacy. On the eve of the election Sherman sent the message to President Lincoln, "I beg to present you with the city of Atlanta." General Sheridan was doing a splendid job of clearing the Shenandoah Valley of "Rebs" and David Farragut was shouting, "Damn the torpedoes, full speed ahead," as he took New Orleans. *Harpers Weekly* told it all with banner headlines following the election, "LONG ABE A LITTLE LONGER". The Union party had pulled it out.

On April 9, 1865, the War Between the States came to a halt when Confederate Robert E. Lee surrendered to Union General U.S. Grant at Appomattox Court House in Virginia. This was the day that President Lincoln had prayed for. It would bring to an end the bloodiest war in which America had ever participated. Now, as President Lincoln said in his second inaugural...with malice toward none, with charity for all let us bind up the nation's wounds, care for the widow and do all that may achieve a just and lasting peace...it was time to embark on humanitarian program and bring our countrymen together once again. President Lincoln was not to realize his postwar plans. It was Good Friday, April 14, 1865, when the President would sit in his booth at Ford's Theatre in Washington, D.C. to take advantage of a well-deserved period of relaxation. John Wilkes Booth, a member of a group that plotted the assassination of the President and his cabinet, fired the fatal shot that ended the life of President Lincoln. Vice President Andrew Johnson now faced the gruesome task of Reconstruction.

The period of Reconstruction was to be a very trying experience for the United States. The war was over but the bitterness lingered. President Johnson found himself in opposition with a group in Congress known as the Radical Republicans who were bent on punishing the South for the past four years of disobedience. The leaders of this group were Thaddeus Stevens of Pennsylvania and Charles Sumner of Massachusetts.

President Johnson attempted to follow Lincoln's plan with some minor changes. In contrast to Stevens' Conquered Province theory and Sumner's State Suicide theory, Lincoln had based his plan on the theory that since the Constitution makes no provision for secession of a state from the Union, they never officially left. It was a rebellion of Individuals, Lincoln asserted, and as President he had the power to pardon individuals. With such diverse attitudes toward handling the Confederate states following the war it became obvious to President Johnson that he would not have many relaxed moments.

Perhaps if Lincoln had lived he might have been able to handle the Radical Republicans. He did possess the inimitable quality of soothing ruffled feathers and accepting half a loaf when a whole loaf was not available. Johnson, however, did not possess these desirable qualities. He fought tooth and nail with the Radical Republicans and the word compromise wasn't in his vocabulary.

Thaddeus Stevens set out to get rid of Johnson by orchestrating a measure known as the Tenure of Office Act which he was sure that the President would veto.

This measure provided that the President could not remove a cabinet member who was appointed by a previous President. The Radical Republicans were aware that the President was about to get rid of his Secretary of War, Edwin Stanton, who was actually a spy for the Radical Republicans. Johnson did veto the measure but his veto was overridden by Congress. President Johnson ignoring a measure which he felt was unconstitutional and in an effort to test its constitutionality, fired Stanton. Thaddeus Stevens, upon learning of the President's action, remarked, "This will cost him the Presidency."

Impeachment proceedings were brought against President Johnson by the House of Representatives as provided in the Constitution. The charges against the President were very flimsy indeed. Feeling that the charge of violating a law passed over his veto might not be adequate enough to bring a conviction, the Radical Republicans added such charges as, "He yelled at us from time to time."

In an impeachment case the Senate of the United States acts as the jury with the Chief Justice of the Supreme Court presiding. At that time there were fifty-four Senators and a two thirds vote was necessary for conviction. The President was spared from being the only President removed from office by a vote of thirty-five to nineteen, one vote short of conviction.

Senator Edmund Ross of Kansas who had been counted on by the Radical Republicans to cast a guilty vote, cast a not guilty vote. Ross' dislike of the President was apparently overshadowed by his respect for the Presidency. It was a courageous act of Senator

Ross but it was to be political suicide for he never again was elected to a government post. Many years later a young Senator from Massachusetts, John F. Kennedy, wrote a book devoted to those who put their conviction above political expediency and entitled it *Profiles in Courage*. A chapter in this book is entitled, "I looked down into my open grave", and is devoted to Senator Ross for the vote he cast in the impeachment of Andrew Johnson.

Johnson completed the unexpired term of Lincoln and ten years later was elected to the U.S. Senate. Upon entering the Senate floor, Johnson received a standing ovation from fellow members who welcomed him as the only Senator elected after having served in the high office of the Presidency. Their reaction undoubtedly influenced by the recent humiliating experience endured by the former President.

With the election of 1868 approaching, the Republicans were aware that many voters became disenchanted with their party largely as a result of the impeachment of Andrew Johnson but also because of the hard money stand they appeared to be married to. To win back these votes and to practically guarantee victory at the polls for many years, they started to "wave the bloody shirt" a strategy that proved very effective in this and subsequent elections.[1]

The most popular man in America at this time was a rumpled cigar-chewing general of the recent war who was regarded by all Union supporters as the one most responsible for winning the war. Ulysses S. Grant who was hailed throughout the Union and lavished with expensive gifts was nominated by the Republican party[2] to represent them for the Presidency in 1868. It mattered very little, if at all, that Grant knew absolutely nothing about politics or that Grant had voted but once in a Presidential election and on that occasion his vote was for the Democratic candidate.

The Democrats selected Horatio Seymour, former governor of New York to head their ticket. The Democrats had no illusions about winning this election but they did severely criticize the Radical Reconstruction Program of the Republicans. Although they were to lose the election to the Republicans, they made a good race of it considering that the blacks were now enfranchised and most southern whites were disenfranchised from voting.

It really didn't take the American public long to bestow the nickname "Useless Grant" on the President. His administration was rocked with scandals such as the United States had never experienced before.

One of the most famous of the "Grant Scandals" was the Gold Conspiracy scandal. Jim Fisk and Jay Gould made the decision to buy up all the gold in circulation and having done this they could dictate the price those wishing to buy gold would have to pay. This scheme would not have worked as long as the government kept putting gold in circulation so Fisk and Gold convinced the President that it would be in the best interest of the country if gold was no longer put in circulation by the government. President Grant reasoned that these successful businessmen were in a better position to discern what was economically best for the country. When it was realized that the government had made a serious mistake the problem was corrected when the government commenced putting gold in circulation once again to bring the price down.

Another scandal involved Secretary of War, William Belknap who granted exclusive rights to trade with the Indians at Fort Sill to a trader in exchange for a bribe of $24,500. When impeachment proceedings against the Secretary of War commenced he immediately resigned and the President accepted his resignation "with regret".

There were other scandals such as the Credit Mobilier scandal, the Erie Railroad scandal, the Congressional Salary Grab, and in New York City the Tweed Ring was responsible for stealing over 200 million dollars from the city treasury.

It is true that President Grant was not knowingly involved with any of these scandals, and it is also true that these illicit activities mirrored the times of the post-war years, but the President has to stand guilty of being incredibly stupid for permitting himself to be so manipulated during this period. It seems that Thomas A. Bailey in his book, *The American Pageant* made an accurate assessment of the Grant period when he referred to it as "The era of good stealings".

Of course the Republicans wanted to stay with a winner. Besides there were some whose pockets were not quite full and they had a lot of good ideas for correcting that problem. When Grant was approached in 1872 to seek a second term he accepted unhesitatingly. Some believed that Grant thought that he was doing a good job.

Most Republicans supported President Grant for a second term, but there were some Republicans who abhorred the corruption that characterized the Grant administration and came out for civil service reform. (Ironically the Republican party had also come out for civil service reform.) This group called themselves Liberal Republicans and chose Horace Greeley, a rather eccentric editor of the New York Tribune. There were many who felt that if the Liberal Republicans used more caution in selecting a candidate in this election, Grant could have been defeated.

The Democratic party relished the split in the Republican party and chose not to nominate a candidate but to throw their support to Greeley in the hope of putting an end to "Grantism" in this election. The Democrats were somewhat confident that their decision would send Grant's campaign back "to the wilderness". This, however, was not to be, the result of the election was a resounding triumph for Grant and a resounding defeat for good, honest government.

There is little question that the most controversial election ever held in the United States occurred in 1876. Many people to this day feel that the election was stolen away from the Democratic party candidate. There is probably some validity to this contention since this view has survived all these years.

In 1876, the Republican party in seeking a candidate to represent them shied away from the movement to nominate the incumbent, Grant, to a third term in order to honor the two term tradition set up by Washington and honored by his predecessors. Instead, they looked to other possible candidates to represent their party.

One possible candidate, James G. Blaine of Maine was considered a front-runner for the candidacy. His campaign was proceeding nicely and it looked very much like he would replace Grant in the White House. The tempo of his campaign slowed and ultimately came to a halt when it was discovered that he had been involved in irregularities with a railroad while serving as Speaker of the House. In his dealings with the railroad he had written incriminating letters and always concluded with "Burn this letter". Instead of burning the letters, the railroad executives filed them away. A clerk in the railway office by the name of Mulligan in going through the files one day was thoroughly shocked when he ran across several of the letters that Blaine had written. When news of this discovery reached Blaine, he immediately went to Mulligan offering to buy the letters. When Mulligan refused, Blaine reportedly begged for the letters and when this, too, failed he asked Mulligan if he could at least look at the letters. Once in his hands, Blaine dashed off with them.

In the meantime a congressional meeting was being held to look into Blaine's alleged irregularities. Blaine appeared before the House with the letters and offered to read them aloud to show that he had done nothing wrong. In reading the letters, Blaine read out of context obviously eliminating the incriminating portions. This was immediately recognized by House members who admonished Blaine to read all or none of the letters. When Blaine refused to divulge the entire contents of the letters, the Republicans started to look elsewhere for their candidate. Another possible candidate being considered was a longtime adversary of Blaine, Roscoe Conkling of New York.

Fearful that neither Blaine nor Conkling would be their wisest choice, The Republicans turned to a virtual unknown, Rutherford B. Hayes, three-time governor of politically potent Ohio, who in political lingo would be called a "dark horse" candidate. The Republicans, in an attempt to squeeze one more President out of the bloody shirt took time to remind the voters that their candidate, Major General Hayes, had been wounded three times during the recent war. To make their platform more palatable to the reformers they included planks calling for civil service reform and an end to the harsh reconstruction of the South. There was also a controversy raging between the cheap money and sound money factions of the nation, so the Republicans put in a plank calling for sound money.

The Democrats put their hopes in a young lawyer, Samuel J. Tilden, who had won great distinction in successfully prosecuting William Marcy Tweed of New York City and thus ending the days of the unscrupulous Tweed Ring. The Democrats were vehemently calling for civil service reform and an end to the presence of federal troops in the South. Of course, the civil service reform plank served to remind the voters of the corrupt, scandal-ridden administration of Republican, U.S. Grant.

To win this election a majority of 185 electoral votes would be needed. The Democrats were extremely confident when Tilden garnered 184 electoral votes as opposed to 165 for Hayes. There were still twenty electoral votes unaccounted for and surely Tilden would be able to acquire one of them; so thought the Democrats. The twenty votes, still unaccounted for were disputed votes from the states of Oregon, Florida, Louisiana and South Carolina. It seems that an elector from Oregon became ineligible but that problem was quickly resolved when another elector was selected. This elector cast his ballot for Hayes. The count now stood at 184-166 in favor of Tilden, the Democratic candidate. The remaining nineteen votes from the states of Florida, Louisiana and South Carolina were being contested because these states were still operating under carpetbag governments.

Both the Democrats and Republicans claimed victory in these states and sent their electors to the state capitals to cast their ballot. (The Democrats argued that the Republicans threw out the votes which they claimed to be fraudulent and the Republicans argued that the Democrats prevented many blacks from exercising their right to vote. Evidence indicates that both the Democrats and Republicans had valid arguments.) The ballots were sealed and, in compliance with the Constitution, sent to the President of the Senate to be counted. Heretofore, it was quite simple—when the votes of the electors were sent to the President of the Senate, he, in the presence of both houses of Congress, opened the votes and counted them. In this instance when the President of the Senate who was a Republican proceeded to count the votes, the Democrats, fully aware that he would count only the votes of the Republican electors in these states raised a constitutional question. They cited Amendment Twelve to the Constitution which states in part:

> …the electors shall meet in their respective states, and vote by ballot for President and Vice President, one of whom, at least, shall not be an inhabitant of the same state with themselves; they shall name in their ballots the person voted for as President, and in distinct ballots the person voted for as Vice President, and they shall make distinct lists of all persons voted for as President and of all persons voted for as Vice President, and of the number of votes for each, which lists they shall sign and certify, and transmit, sealed, to the seat of government of the United States; the president of the Senate shall, in the presence of the Senate and House of Representatives, open all the certificates and the votes shall then be counted…

But counted by whom? The Constitution does not state that the President of the Senate shall count the votes.

The election was decided when a special electoral commission of fifteen was appointed to decide the outcome. Five from the Senate, five from the House of Representatives, and five from the Supreme Court. In the 1874 election the Democrats won control of the House, the Senate was still controlled by the Republicans, and the Supreme Court comprised both

Democrats and Republicans plus one Independent. The following is the makeup of the original electoral commission:

House of Representatives: 3 Democrats, 2 Republicans

U.S. Senate: 2 Democrats, 3 Republicans

Supreme Court: 2 Democrats, 2 Republicans, 1 Independent

Prior to the voting of the commission, the one Independent in the Supreme Court, David Davis, was elected to the Senate and that rendered him ineligible to serve on the commission. All of the remaining justices in the Supreme Court were Republicans and so a Republican, Joseph Bradley, was selected to take Davis' place. Voting strictly along party lines, the commission gave the election to Hayes by a vote of 8-7.

To appease the Democrats, and in an effort to have Hayes' inauguration devoid of incident, the Republicans promised that one of the President's first moves would be to remove the last of the federal troops from the South. The Democrats' only consolation from this election was to see the radical Republican program of reconstruction come to an end. This was accomplished in 1877. To prevent a reoccurrence of the problem created in this election, Congress, in 1887, passed the Electoral Count Act which states that in a future situation where duplicate sets of returns should result in any state, the Governor of the state will decide which of the returns are the legitimate ones to be sent to the nation's capital.

Rutherford B. Hayes' tenure in the White House was not to be a thrilling experience for the President. The Democrats never lost sight of the manner in which Hayes was elected and kept constantly referring to him as "old 8-7". Since the Democrats controlled the House during the entire term of the President and controlled the Senate half that time, they proved to be no "rubber stamp" for the President's programs.

Hayes proved to be a champion for civil service reform much to the chagrin of the radical Republicans. As promised, he did remove the last federal troops from the South. He also signed the Bland-Allison Act which required the government to buy and coin between two and four million dollars worth of silver each month. This measure would satisfy the cheap money people but did little to bring applause from his own party members.

During Hayes' presidency a split developed in the ranks of the Republican party. One faction was led by Roscoe Conkling and called themselves Stalwarts[3]. The Stalwarts were the "old guard", anti-reform Republicans who would be delighted to see Ulysses Simpson Grant serve once again in that exalted office of the Presidency. Another faction was led by James G. Blaine, and they called themselves Half-breeds. They were mildly interested in reform and were wildly in love with Blaine. The Mugwumps, another faction of Republicans, were extremely interested in reform. Probably the most face-saving decision the President made was to announce, before the 1880 presidential convention, that he would not be available for the nomination of the Republican party.

As the election of 1880 approached, the Stalwarts were hard at work trying to get former President Grant to run again and return to the "good old days". Grant showed more than a slight willingness to run. After all, he said, he wouldn't be breaking the two-term tradition because he wouldn't be serving three consecutive terms. James G. Blaine bitterly opposed the nomination of Grant. He would, he confessed, accept the nomination if it were offered to him. Unable to agree on Grant or Blaine, the Republicans chose a dark horse candidate, James A. Garfield of Ohio. Garfield had been a general of the Union Army but that didn't hold the romance it once held; the bloody shirt by now had turned a pale pink. To reconcile the Stalwarts and hopefully to reunite their party the Republicans selected Chester A. Arthur as their vice presidential choice.

The Democrats nominated Winfield S. Hancock of Pennsylvania, also a general of the Union Army. Neither party faced up to the real issues confronting the nation. The Republicans were urging a protective tariff for revenue purposes only. Civil service reform was mentioned by both parties—feebly by the Republicans, enthusiastically by the Democrats.

The election results were close, indeed. Garfield won in the electoral vote 214-155 but out of nine million votes cast, he polled less than 10,000 more votes than Hancock. Conkling was infuriated when Garfield named James G. Blaine his Secretary of State. To add insult to injury, Garfield appointed an adversary of Conkling's to the post of collector of the port of New York.

President Garfield was not to serve more than four months. He would become the second President to be assassinated while in office. He was shot in a railway station by a disappointed office-seeker, Charles J. Guiteau. When Giteau shot the President he exclaimed, "I am a Stalwart; Arthur is now President of the United States." At this point it is difficult to determine whether the people were more shocked at the death of Garfield or the ascension of Arthur to the presidency.

It was a sad commentary that a President should lose his life because of his failure to make an appointment to government service. Paradoxically, the President was assassinated because of the spoils system while, indeed, it was his death that led to the passage of the Pendleton Civil Service Act which requires competitive exams for certain government jobs which appear on the "classified list". President Arthur supported the Pendleton Act and placed approximately ten per cent of all government jobs on the classified list. (Subsequent presidents have substantially added to the list over the years.)

Chester A. Arthur proved to be a better President than people expected or probably deserved from that former collector of the port of New York. He did such a good job that he alienated both the Stalwart arid Half-breed elements of his party and completely destroyed any chance he might have had for the Republican party nomination in 1884. Arthur truly believed in his doctrine, "He serves his party best who serves his country best."

In 1884 the stage was set for the dirtiest, most mud-slinging campaign for the presidency this nation has ever experienced. For a while both candidates wondered whether they were running for the presidency or the penitentiary. It was an election where the voter was forced to choose between the private immorality of the Democratic candidate or the public dishonesty of the Republican candidate. As the outcome of the election is analyzed it becomes apparent that the voters had a difficult time deciding between the two; private immorality and public dishonesty almost ran a dead heat.

President Arthur indicated to his fellow Republicans that he would like to stay President but he had alienated his early supporters, the Stalwarts, with his reform measure. At any rate, the Half-Breeds were now in control of the party and it was looking pretty good for James G. Blaine. Save honesty, Blaine had many of the characteristics one would look for in a presidential candidate. He made a striking appearance and was referred to as "the plumed knight". The logical choice of the Republicans was Blaine as they met in the city of Chicago. He did not, however, have the unified support of the party and this ultimately cost him the election. The faction of his party that opposed him called themselves Mugwumps, an Indian name meaning "holier than thou". They were disenchanted with the corrupt dealings Blaine was reported to have had while serving in the capacity of Speaker of the House.

The Democrats who hadn't had a President in the White House in twenty-eight years looked upon this election as a golden opportunity to regain some self-respect. This is the year to pull it off, they reasoned, with the Republican party displaying such a tainted candidate. In contrast to Blaine, the Democrats nominated the reform governor of New York, Stephen Grover Cleveland. Cleveland was a man of high integrity, thoroughly honest and highly principled. The Democrats referred to him as "Grover the Good".

It was inevitable as the presidential campaign ground its way toward the election that the Mulligan Letters once more would make their presence felt. The Democrats made these letters the focus of their attention when in their torchlight parades they chanted as they marched down the busy streets of America, "James G. Blaine, James G. Blaine, the continental liar from the state of Maine, BURN THESE LETTERS, BURN THESE LETTERS!"

The Republicans now felt that they had to put Cleveland under the microscope. Nobody could be that good, they reasoned. They put their best men on the case to look into every conceivable aspect of Cleveland's life. EUREKA! shouted the Republicans when it was discovered that Cleveland had earlier seduced a widow and was now the proud father of an eight year old boy.

The Democrats, upon learning of the Republicans' discovery charged Cleveland to assume the role of a master politician and lie about it. "Tell the truth" was Cleveland's instructions to his campaigners. He told them that he had cared for the child and had not a thing to be ashamed of. Reverend Henry Ward Beecher inadvertently cost Cleveland some votes with his misguided support when he stated, "If every New Yorker who violated the seventh commandment voted for Cleveland, he would win by a 200,000 plurality." Nonetheless, the Republicans were now to give the Democrats a taste of their own medicine when, in their torchlight parades, they chanted, "Hey, Ma! Where's my Pa!" (The Democrats were later able to answer, "Gone to the White House, Ha! Ha! Ha!")

As election day neared, the Republicans were running scared. It would take a united Republican party to defeat the Democrats they felt. They knew the chances weren't very good, but nevertheless they approached the Mugwumps and asked if they could see fit to support Blaine for the presidency. Their answer was swift and resolute, "We do not engage in criminal practice." So much for the Mugwumps, the Republicans reasoned.

On the very eve of the election an incident occurred that all but sealed the fate of the Republican party. At a dinner given in honor of Blaine one of the speakers, a Reverend Burchard, stated that he personally would never vote for a president whose antecedents were a party of "Rum, Romanism, and Rebellion." It would have been real shrewd if Blaine had paid attention to the Reverend (some say that a very tiring campaign resulted in Blaine grabbing a few winks.) Whatever the reason, Blaine did not clarify his position on that point. This statement was a slap in the face to all Catholics and it so happened that New York was to become the pivotal state in this election and New York voters were well represented by Catholics. Blaine's wife was a Catholic and while it may appear that Blaine did not share the conviction of Reverend Burchard, his silence made him appear suspect in the eyes of the Catholic voter. As it turned out, Cleveland won New York by a meager 1149 votes and with New York, the presidency. It is also extremely important to note that the Mugwumps voted for Cleveland in this election.

President Cleveland believed that "a public office is a public trust." He doubled the classified list much to the disappointment of fellow Democrats who after twenty-eight years were eager to cash in on the spoils of victory.

A somewhat strange situation faced President Cleveland as he entered the White House. The government was faced with an embarrassing surplus in the treasury. The surplus came mainly from the high protective tariff levied on imports during the Civil War and which was continued following the war. The surplus was an evil because the money should have been in circulation to benefit a growing economy.

In an attempt to aid the government shed its embarrassment over the surplus two remedies were tossed about; the G.A.R., (an acronym for Grand Army of the Republic), came up with hundreds of pension bills for veterans of the Civil War. These bills were passed by Congress and sent to the President for his signature. The President, in investigating these bills found out that many of them were for deserters from the Union Army, some of the bills were for persons who never served in the armed forces of the United States, and some were for veterans who became disabled at their workplace and not from any service connected injury. Cleveland vetoed over 200 such bills and in so doing incurred the wrath of the G.A.R. who immediately branded him as anti-veteran. (Cleveland did not serve in the armed forces.) This charge, however, was unfair for the President had signed hundreds of legitimate pension bills into law.

The other remedy suggested was to lower the tariff. Cleveland, against the advice of his party, fought for a lower tariff. He was vehemently opposed by the Republicans and industry who argued that Cleveland was in favor of free trade (absence of any import duty). This tariff proposal of Cleveland's was to play a major role in his reelection bid for the presidency in 1888.

As the election of 1888 approached, the Democrats found it necessary to renominate Cleveland to a second term. They were not ecstatic with his reform programs nor his feelings toward tariff reform, but he was the incumbent and there was no other candidate available who would stand the slightest chance of winning the election.

James G. Blaine still harbored hopes of becoming President. Cleveland had come under rather severe criticism during his administration and Blaine relished the thought of switching the results of the 1884 election around. He was, however, cognizant that people had not forgotten the charges leveled against him in 1884 and was sure that they would be resurrected if he chose to run again. Besides, he felt that his chances of receiving the nomination of his party were meager at best. He did recommend Benjamin Harrison of Indiana whom the Republicans nominated at their convention. Benjamin Harrison was the grandson of former President William Henry Harrison and this would have to work in their favor reasoned the Republicans.

The big issue during this campaign was the tariff. The Democrats felt that a low tariff for revenue purposes was all that was required while the Republicans demanded a protective tariff to keep cheaper foreign products from competing with American-made products.

Once again the Irish vote of New York was to play a significant role in the outcome of an election. It seems that a dispute between the U.S. and Great Britain was raging over fishing rights and Cleveland was purported to lean toward the British point of view. The Irish, always eager to twist the British lion's tail, became disenchanted with the Democratic candidate although the charges of being pro British were trumped up against Cleveland.

The Democrats saw their incumbent go down to defeat. Benjamin Harrison received 233 electoral votes to 168 electoral votes for Cleveland. In the popular vote Cleveland gathered slightly over 100,000 votes more than did Harrison. The popular choice of the people went down to defeat; another indictment against the electoral system of electing a President.

During the administration of Benjamin Harrison measures were passed which were not traditionally Republican in nature. In 1890 the Sherman Anti-Trust Act was enacted into law which had as its main purpose the regulation of the conduct of big business by prohibiting monopolies and other questionable business practices. In the same year the Sherman Silver

Purchase Act was passed which required the government to buy and coin four and one half million ounces of silver each month—not nearly enough to satisfy the cheap money advocates but clearly not a measure characteristic of the Republican party. The one measure, typically Republican, passed during this administration was the McKinley tariff which raised the tariff rates on imports from 38% to 50%.

The Republicans were weakened for the election of 1892. The reformers were anything but satisfied with the measures enacted into law during the Harrison administration and the farmers were more than mildly upset with the higher prices resulting from the McKinley tariff. In the 1890 congressional elections the number of Republicans in the House of Representatives was cut in half by the Democratic landslide.

Farmer alliances were formed throughout the agrarian sections of the United States to provide an alternative to the two-party system which the farmers felt were not truly representing their interests.

In 1891, a new party was formed consisting mainly of farmers but also laborers and others discontented with the Republican and Democratic parties. This new party which called itself the Populist Party met in Omaha, Nebraska, and nominated as their candidate, James B. Weaver. Their platform called for free and unlimited coinage of silver at the ratio of 16:1, (sixteen ounces of silver for each ounce of gold). In addition, the Populists called for direct election of Senators, (Senators had been selected by the House of Representatives and was referred to as the "rich man's club".) A secret ballot, the initiative, referendum and recall, a graduated income tax and a postal savings system.

A driving force behind the farmers' political revolt was a woman, Mary Elizabeth Lease of Kansas who led a fiery crusade to organize the farmers. She repeatedly charged the farmers "to raise less corn and more hell". In one of her fiery speeches she proclaimed, "Wall Street owns the country. It is no longer a government of the people, by the people and for the people, but a government of Wall Street, by Wall Street and for Wall Street." (Wall Street is the financial center of the United States located in New York City.) The Saturday Evening Post in commenting on the crusade of Mrs. Lease suggested that we should not admit any more states into the Union until we civilized Kansas.

The Republican party renominated Benjamin Harrison to a second term. Their platform vigorously defended the McKinley tariff as essential to the welfare of the United States.

Grover Cleveland was nominated by the Democratic party for the third time and their platform continued its attack on the high tariff Republicans.

Rather harmful to the Republican cause were a series of strikes which plagued the United States and somewhat defeated the argument of the Republicans that the McKinley tariff was good for the working man. The most serious of the strikes and by far the one most damaging to Harrison was the famous Homestead Steel strike in Homestead, Pennsylvania. Pinkerton detectives were originally used by the company to smash the strike and later the Governor of Pennsylvania called in troops to break up the strike and the union.

Stephen Grover Cleveland was to win the election easily and with this victory President Cleveland was to become the only President elected to two non-consecutive terms.

The Populist party was to make a remarkable showing for a minor party. They accumulated over one million votes and amassed twenty-two electoral votes. The popularity of the Populists did not go unnoticed by either the Democratic or Republican parties. They became acutely aware that this new party was more than a few disgruntled farmers banding together. It is also interesting to note at this point that the following laws and amendments to the Constitution now govern us and that it was the Populist party that first brought the need for them to the attention of the American voter:

1903—Los Angeles adopts the recall.
1910—Postal savings system started.
1913—Sixteenth amendment to the Constitution calling for a graduated income tax.
1913—Seventeenth amendment to the Constitution calling for direct election of Senators.

The Populist movement did indeed fulfill the traditionally important role of third parties by bringing new issues to national attention until adopted by major parties.

President Cleveland was faced with a serious labor dispute when the American Railway Union under the leadership of Eugene V. Debs called for a strike against the Pullman Palace Car Company in Pullman, Illinois. Workers refused to handle any train with a Pullman car attached. The President decided to send federal troops to Illinois to end the strike when Governor Altgeld of Illinois refused to intervene. Cleveland used the argument that the mails were not going through—a charge that was vehemently denied. In any event this action of President Cleveland incurred the wrath of organized labor who viewed the President as anti-labor.

A serious financial crisis occurred in 1893 when businesses were forced to close their doors and banks throughout the United States failed. It became known as the panic of 1893. The problem occurred when the Sherman Silver Purchase Act was passed during the administration of President Benjamin Harrison. This measure had the effect of putting the United States on a bimetallistic standard which provided silver and gold as the backing for the nation's currency. Since this measure required the United States to buy and coin four and one half million ounces of silver each month it caused the value of silver to drop considerably. As a result Gresham's Law[4] prevailed when more and more citizens started to redeem their silver bank notes for gold coins. If this trend were to continue the United States would be faced with the devastating prospect of having to go on the silver standard which would translate into economic disaster for the nation.

President Cleveland attempted to avert such a disaster by calling a special session of Congress for the purpose of repealing the Sherman Silver Purchase Act. Lobbyists worked feverishly on behalf of the cheap money people to prevent this from happening but common sense prevailed and the act was repealed. The problem of a gold shortage wasn't corrected by this Congressional act but it was corrected when President Cleveland accepted the offer of a group of bankers led by J.P. Morgan to loan gold to the government in exchange for government bonds as security for the loan.

The action taken by President Cleveland did avert serious financial consequences. The people now regained confidence in the government monetary judgment and the run on the gold reserves ended. Many, however, criticized the high rate of interest paid to the bankers by the government.

The nation was now split between the "sound money" gold standard people and the "cheap money" silver people as the election of 1896 approached. The Republican party would become the representatives of the "sound money" groups and the Democrats would represent the "cheap money" interests.

William McKinley of Ohio, author of the McKinley tariff of 1890, was selected by the Republicans to represent them in the election. McKinley was known to be a great supporter of big business and sure to be a great supporter of the "sound money" interests. He was fortunate to have as his friend and campaign manager Marcus Alonzo Hanna, "maker of Presidents", and a multimillionaire in his own right. Hanna saw to it that McKinley received the nomination in St. Louis on the first ballot by his generous outpouring of money—much of it his own.

The Democrats didn't know who to support as the convention time approached. The party was in disarray; they had turned against Cleveland and his "ill fated" administration replete with the Pullman Strike, The Panic of 1893, and the J.P. Morgan deal. The silver "cheap money" people dominated this convention but they had no leader to represent them.

The situation at the Democratic convention in Chicago was made to order for a young man from Nebraska named William Jennings Bryan. "The Boy Orator of the Platte" seized upon the confusion at the convention to get to the podium and deliver what has come down to us in history as the famous "Cross of Gold" speech.

In his speech representing the silver interests of the country he remarked:

> You come to us and tell us that the great cities are in favor of the gold standard; we reply that the great cities rest upon our broad and fertile prairies. Burn down your cities and leave our farms, and your cities will spring up again as if by magic; but destroy our farms and the grass will grow in the streets of every city in the country. Having behind us the producing masses of this nation and the world, supported by the commercial interests, the laboring interests, and the toilers everywhere, we will answer their demand for a gold standard by

saying to them: You shall not press down on the brow of labor this crown of thorns, you shall not crucify mankind upon a cross of gold.

Even before Bryan concluded his speech pandemonium broke out at the convention. They would look no further for a leader; they had found the splendid orator and personable standard bearer who would debate the "sound money" people into submission.

The Populist Party saw nothing but disadvantage in putting up their own candidate in 1896. The Democrats had taken their major plank calling for free and unlimited coinage of silver at the ratio of 16:1. They chose instead to support the Democratic candidate for the Presidency but they did nominate a Vice Presidential candidate to let the people know that they were alive and well. The rest of their platform once again called for direct election of Senators, graduated income tax, and direct legislation through the initiative and referendum.

Besides the monetary consideration addressed by all parties the question of an overseas empire became paramount, especially with respect to Hawaii. The Democrats were opposed to any overseas expansion while the Republicans looked forward to the annexation of Hawaii and perhaps acquiring other Pacific and Caribbean possessions.

William McKinley was elected President of the United States in 1896 collecting 271 electoral votes to Bryan's 176.

There is little doubt that the treasury chest of the Republicans played a major role in the outcome of the election. The Republicans, through the efforts of Mark Hanna, raised a treasure chest of $3,500,000, in comparison to the $300,000 expended by the Democrats.

Also significant in this campaign were the divergent styles used by the leading candidates. Bryan "stumped the country" making a total of 600 speeches in fourteen weeks while McKinley carried on a "front porch campaign". On the eve of the election factory workers were given their pay and informed that they were not to return to work if McKinley was defeated, there would be no jobs for them. It is highly suspect that this tactic employed by business played more than a small role in the defeat of Bryan.

President McKinley was fortunate to have the shortage of gold in the United States resolved when gold was discovered in the Klondike region of Alaska and equally flattering to the President was the prosperous period enjoyed by business manifested by U.S. Steel becoming the first billion dollar business. The Sherman Anti-Trust Act was not enforced during the administration of President McKinley and thus the practices of businesses did not come under the scrutiny of the government.

Probably highlighting the McKinley administration was a "splendid little war" between the United States and Spain, the Spanish-American War. This war was to last slightly over 120 days but long enough for thousands of young American boys to fall victim to malaria and yellow fever, (these diseases became more of an enemy than any bullet fired by the enemy), and long enough for the United States to acquire a vast Pacific empire as well as to make the Caribbean an "American lake".

The trouble started in Cuba when the Cubans grew tired of seeing their country being exploited by the Spanish. They saw much of the wealth produced in Cuba leave the country and not used to improve the deplorable conditions that plagued the island. The Cubans revolted and this was to cause great concern in the United States to investors who had a total of 50 million dollars invested in the island and the loss of 100 million dollars in annual trade greatly concerned the United States.

The yellow press had a heyday during the period preceding the declaration of war on Spain by the United States. Two rival New York newspapers were competing for increased circulation and the situation in Cuba played right into their hands. Joseph Pulitzer, editor and publisher of the *New York World* and William Randolph Hearst, editor and publisher of the *New York Journal* were playing a game of "can you top this?" When one of these newspapers would carry an account, usually very gruesome accounts of mistreatment of the Cubans, particularly innocent children, the other rival would "go one better" by depicting Spaniards walking around with rifles on their shoulders with babies impaled on their bayonets. It worked, both newspapers' circulation skyrocketed during this period. At one point William Randolph Hearst sent his cartoonist Frederick Remington to Cuba to draw pictures of atrocities he observed.

Unable to find any such situation, he informed his editor who promptly sent the wire to Remington, "You supply the pictures, I'll supply the war."

The sinking of the U.S. Battleship Maine in Havana Harbor was the immediate cause of the U.S. declaration of war against Spain in 1898. In the minds of most Americans there was little doubt that the Spaniards had sunk the battleship, but to this date the cause of the sinking is not resolved. There is, however, much credence given to the theory that one of the boilers exploded in the engine room of the ship, a disaster which was not that uncommon aboard vessels during that period of time. This was the explanation given by the Spanish when they argued that the shape of the hull indicated that the explosion took place from within. This theory conflicted with the American inquiry group that argued that the explosion took place outside the vessel.

It is somewhat paradoxical that at the time the U.S. declared war on Spain, Congress enacted the Teller Resolutions which stated that the United States was not interested in an inch of territory and yet, as a result of the war, the U.S. acquired a vast overseas empire.

William McKinley was renominated by the Republican party in 1900. As a running mate the party chose Theodore Roosevelt—not because of his daring exploits during the recent war when he led his Roughriders on the famous charge up San Juan Hill, but to shut him up. Roosevelt, as Governor of New York often spoke out against Republican policies and such criticism was widely covered by the newspapers as newsworthy. By putting "Teddy" in the Vice

Presidential spot, reasoned the Republican hierarchy, nothing he said (as a Vice President) would be newsworthy. Mark Hanna, who intensely disliked Roosevelt felt that this strategy was very dangerous since it would put Roosevelt a heartbeat away from the Presidency.

The Democrats once again nominated William Jennings Bryan. Even though the issue of cheap money did not hold the attraction it once did, the Democrats inserted it as one of their platform planks.

The main issue upon which the Democrats and Republicans disagreed was that of expansion. The Republicans were very proud of the acquisitions made as a result of the recent war, but the Democrats saw no need for additional territory. A common question in the minds of many Republicans as well as Democrats was, "Now that we have acquired the Philippines what are we going to do with them?" It was even suggested that we give them back to Spain.

The Populists once again threw their support behind the Democratic candidate, Bryan, rather than to split the vote on issues upon which both the Democrats and Populists agreed.

The Socialists made their debut in Presidential elections by nominating their new convert, Eugene V. Debs.

McKinley defeated Bryan more convincingly than he did in 1896. Mark Hanna, delighted that his protégé was reelected was greatly grieved six months later when the President was assassinated by a half-crazed anarchist. "My God, that damned cowboy is now President," exclaimed Hanna.

Conservative Republicans who feared that "Teddy" would continue his progressive ways were not to be shocked by a change in style by Roosevelt; he continued to be his "own man" and indeed ushered in a new era in American politics, The Progressive Era.

As the youngest President ever in our nation's history (John F. Kennedy was the youngest elected President) he earned a reputation as the "trust buster" by prosecuting violators of the Sherman Anti-Trust Law. He also set a precedent in the Coal Strike of 1902 by siding with labor in the dispute centered in the Commonwealth of Pennsylvania. He acquired the Canal Zone for the United States. "I took Panama" was a boast of Roosevelt's to indicate how he maneuvered a rebellion in Panama which led to the passage of the Hay-Bunau-Varilla treaty authorizing the building of the Panama Canal by the United States, and it was he who coined the phrase "muckrakers" in assailing those writers of the period who published the evils of our society found in such areas as the meat packing plants of Chicago, the slum conditions existing within our cities, and even within the Senate of the U.S.

Absolutely nothing would have pleased the conservative Republicans more than to dump Roosevelt as the 1904 election approached. To do this would certainly have been counter-productive for the Republicans since Roosevelt had become close to an idol to many Americans. His only rival for his nomination would have been Mark Hanna but Hanna was unable to make a President of himself. He died in 1904 before the convention got under way. Roosevelt was nominated by acclamation at the Chicago convention.

The Bryan movement lost its glitter at the Democratic convention. The Democrats sought a "safe and sane" candidate and they thought that they had found him in Alton B. (Judge) Parker of New York. The Socialist candidate, Eugene Victor Debs, was to make his second of five attempts for the Presidency.

Theodore Roosevelt promised the voter nothing more and nothing less than a "square deal" and judging from what Roosevelt had delivered during his past administration the people came to expect nothing less. Roosevelt won a resounding victory defeating Judge Parker 336 to 140 in electoral votes. No longer a President "by accident" Roosevelt continued his vigorous reform programs and saw such measures as the Meat Inspection Act and the Pure Food and Drug Act enacted into law. The Hepburn Act put teeth in the Interstate Commerce Act, a measure designed to regulate the railroad industry.

Roosevelt felt that the United States needed "a strong President but not a perpetual one" and declined to accept the nomination of his party in 1908. With the exception of big business and others opposed to his reform programs, Roosevelt was extremely popular with the masses and there seems little doubt that he would have won the nomination of his party and the support of the voting public should he have decided to continue the "bully time" he was enjoying as President. Instead he hand-picked his Secretary of War, 350 pound William Howard Taft, most likely to carry out his programs. "Teddy" saw to it that Taft received the nomination on the first ballot and then proceeded to pack his gear for his hunting safari in Africa confident that the country was in good hands.

The Democrats, once again, chose William Jennings Bryan as their candidate. The Bryan supporters had gained support of the party and throughout the campaign complained bitterly that the Republicans had stolen many of the programs initiated by their candidate. It is true that many of Bryan's recommendations were enacted into law during the Roosevelt years causing Bryan on one occasion to remark that he was the only man in America to rule the country without the benefit of having been elected President.

The Socialist party once again nominated Eugene V. Debs to head their ticket. He would represent the Party again in the election of 1912. In 1920, imprisoned under the Espionage Act for hindering the war effort he made his final appearance as the Socialist candidate; as Prisoner No. 2253 of the Atlanta Penitentiary he polled 919,799.

William Howard Taft would become the twenty-seventh President of the United States defeating Bryan 321 to 162 in the electoral count. This election would mark the last time that William Jennings Bryan would seek the Presidency, and the first time that the American Federation of Labor would support the entire slate of a political party. They supported the entire slate of the Democratic party because they felt the Republicans were not doing enough for organized labor. Prior to 1908 the A F of L crossed party lines and supported the candidates friendly to labor.

The tariff had been a major issue in the election of 1908. The Democrats called for a lower tariff and the Republicans called for a revision of the tariff which was translated to mean a lower tariff by the electorate. During the administration of Taft, however, the Payne-Aldrich tariff was enacted which actually raised the tariff on many items. The public felt betrayed by the Republicans by not lowering the tariff. President Taft made a rather serious error in judgment when he not only defended the Payne-Aldrich Tariff but referred to it as the best law the Republican party ever passed.

Another incident occurred during the administration of Taft which was to alienate the progressive element of the party as well as all proponents of conservation of the country's natural resources. The incident was referred to as the Ballinger-Pinchot controversy and involved the selling of timber lands and water power sites which had been in the federal reserve.

Ballinger was the Secretary of the Interior who favored the selling of the reserves and Pinchot was the Chief Forrester (appointed by Roosevelt) who opposed the sale. During the controversy President Taft supported Ballinger, fired Pinchot, and the sale was consummated.

"Teddy" Roosevelt in supporting Taft for the Presidency in 1908 had maintained that Taft would be the candidate most likely to carry out his programs. He, upon hearing of the Payne-Aldrich Tariff and the Ballinger-Pinchot controversy, was heard to remark that Taft was carrying his programs out to the garbage dump. Convinced that a madman was at the helm of the United States government, Roosevelt cut short his hunting safari in Africa to return home and "throw his hat in the ring". He would enter the race wrest control of the Republican convention away from Taft and put this nation on the right course again.

When Theodore Roosevelt left the United States for his hunting safari cartoonists sketched scenes of Americans at the dock, handkerchiefs to their eyes waving goodbye to their former President and friend as the children clutched their teddy bears. Such was the scene in reality when Roosevelt departed the United States and it's quite understandable that Roosevelt did not expect any major obstacles at the Republican convention of 1912. However, when Roosevelt attempted to gain the nomination at the convention he was to become painfully aware of the advantages of the incumbency. Taft became the favorite of the Republican delegates. Roosevelt, in one of his inimitable tirades, stormed out of the convention "mad as a bull moose" and split the Republican party by running on the Progressive or Bull Moose ticket for the Presidency in 1912.

The Democrats delighted over the split in the Republican party and anticipating that the Americans were desiring reforms selected as their candidate the reform Governor of New Jersey, Thomas Woodrow Wilson. Wilson had served as President of Princeton University and thus was quickly labeled the "Princeton Schoolmaster". Wilson was offering the American people a "New Freedom" if elected in contrast to the "New Nationalism" being offered by Roosevelt.

The election results brought an overwhelming victory for Wilson and the Democrats in the electoral votes:

Wilson—Democrat, 435 electoral votes
Roosevelt—Progressive, 88 electoral votes
Taft—Republican, 8 electoral votes

Once again it must be noted that Wilson was to become a minority President.

During Wilson's administration some notable accomplishments were made on the domestic scene which were to have a lasting effect on future America: The seventeenth amendment was added to the Constitution which provided for direct election of Senators by the electorate; the Underwood Tariff was enacted into law and was the first major reduction in the tariff since the War Between the States; the Federal Reserve Act was passed which provided for the Federal Reserve System, and the Panama Canal was opened to traffic. The reform Governor of New Jersey proved to be a reform President of the United States.

The Democrats were very proud of the accomplishments made during the Wilson administration and they were certain that the American electorate shared their feelings. The Democratic convention meeting in St. Louis enthusiastically renominated Wilson to a second term and found that the slogan "He kept us out of the War" had a nice ring to it since the foremost wish of Americans was to stay out of the conflict which was raging in Europe.

Roosevelt was the choice of the Progressive ticket once again but mindful of the damaging effect the Republican rupture of 1912 had on the outcome of the election refused the offer.

There were those at the Republican convention meeting in Chicago that longed to get "Teddy" on the ticket in 1916 but there were many more delegates there still smarting from the action of Teddy in the 1912 election to block any such move. The convention decided upon Supreme Court Justice Charles Evans Hughes, former Governor of New York, to discipline the school master.

During the campaign the Republicans assailed the Underwood Tariff and argued that Wilson was bungling foreign affairs. Wilson was quite content to run on his record and was particularly proud that the United States was not involved in the European War.

The results of the election were close indeed. Wilson did nose out Hughes by acquiring 277 electoral votes to 254 for Hughes. Despite the closeness of the election Wilson took particular pride in defeating a united Republican party and was comforted with the knowledge that he was no longer a minority President.

The highlight of Wilson's second term was U.S. entrance into World War I. It became next to impossible to stay out of the European war following the sinking of the British liner, Lusitania, by a German U-Boat with the loss of over one hundred American lives. In his war message to Congress Wilson proclaimed the war to be "A war to end all wars" and a war "to make the world safe for democracy". It proved to be neither.

On the eleventh hour of the eleventh day of the eleventh month in 1918 the last shot of World War I had been fired. The war was over, the allies had won and the boys would be coming home again. It now remained to draw up a peace treaty officially ending the war. Such a treaty would be drawn up in Paris, France.

During the war President Wilson had drawn up the conditions upon which the Allies would accept Germany's surrender. These conditions were set down in the 14 Points. The 14 Points, Wilson felt, would be the fairest and the most equitable way of arranging for a post war Europe and setting guidelines that, if followed, would greatly lessen the chances of another global war.

President Wilson was to experience serious difficulties both at home and abroad in getting his peace program accepted. During the war the European allies had entered into secret treaties that would decide the fate of post-war Europe and these treaties did not remotely resemble the program laid down in Wilson's 14 Points. At home the President had alienated the Republicans by his so-called "October Appeal" in which he asked the American people to return a Democratic Congress in the Congressional election of 1918. Normally such a request of the voters would be expected but this was not a normal situation. All throughout the war there was a political truce between the Democrats and Republicans. The Republicans supported the President's every move in bringing the European conflict to an end. The "October Appeal" broke the truce and the Republicans were not to forgive the President for his "callous disregard" of the Republican party support during those critical years. The American voters were not taken in at all by this appeal; when election day came a Republican Congress was elected.

President Wilson made other serious errors in judgment during the period immediately following the war. In selecting the peace commission to represent the United States in Paris the Republicans had only token representation. This was particularly annoying to the Republicans since they now controlled Congress. The announcement by the President that he personally was going to attend the peace conference in Paris was extremely opposed by Americans who felt that the President's responsibility was to stay at home and help to iron out the problems facing a post-war America.

The only thing that President Wilson was to salvage from his trip to Paris was the League of Nations, the 14th point. On all other issues he was forced to compromise. The Germans who had surrendered on the basis of Wilson's 14 Points were very bitter and felt that they had been betrayed - one of the arguments used by Adolph Hitler in 1933 when he rose to power in Germany.

Upon returning home it was now incumbent upon the President to win U.S. approval for the League and this was not to happen. The Republicans led by Henry Cabot Lodge and known as the "irreconcilables" refused to accept membership in the League. It was a twist of irony that the League was a brainstorm of the American President and that the United States seriously hampered the effectiveness of the organization by refusing to become a member.

Woodrow Wilson had fought an uphill battle to win support for the League. He went directly to the public in a nationwide three week speaking tour. During this time he suffered a paralytic stroke and remained an invalid until his death in 1924.

According to the Democratic party the election of 1920 was to become a "solemn referendum" in which the American voter would endorse the League by giving the Democratic party a landslide victory. As their Presidential candidate they chose James M. Cox, Governor of Ohio and newspaper editor. Their Vice Presidential choice fell upon a young, handsome, energetic New Yorker and former Assistant Secretary of the Navy, Franklin D. Roosevelt.

The Democrats in this election campaign were fighting hard to make former President Wilson's last days fulfilled by pushing for U.S. membership in the League. The Democrats, however, were seriously hampered by a series of strikes that broke out in the United States. Things were not too harmonious on the "home front".

The Republicans felt that the times did not require them to search too diligently for a superlative candidate. A second-rater would do nicely against a party that had all but destroyed themselves domestically and in foreign relations. For the Democrats to continue to push for the League would be counterproductive reasoned the Republican "brass". The "smoke-filled room" candidate of the Republican party was Warren G. Harding, Senator of Ohio and as in the case of the Democratic candidate, a newspaper editor. Their search for a Vice Presidential running mate ended when they decided upon Calvin "Silent Cal" Coolidge, Governor of Massachusetts who was made famous by his role in the Boston Police strike of 1919. As the Governor of Massachusetts during this strike he made the famous statement, "There is no right to strike against the public safety by anyone, anywhere, anytime." He then called out the state militia to crush the strike.

For a war-weary America the Democrats didn't offer anything refreshing in their platform. The Republicans, however were calling for "A return to normalcy" a very palatable offering since the Americans were disenchanted with affairs of Europe and longed to get back to normal times. The election results revealed an overwhelming victory for Harding and normal living with Harding receiving 404 electoral votes to 127 for Cox. The Republicans were correct— the times didn't require a first-rater to defeat the Democrats.

Significant in this election were that women voted for the first time in a national election owing to the recently ratified nineteenth amendment to the Constitution and that the first commercial broadcasting radio station in America, KDKA in Pittsburgh, Pennsylvania, broadcast the election results for the first time in history.

Notable during the administration of Warren G. Harding was the appointment of Charles G. Dawes as the first Director of the Budget. Also in an effort to control the naval building race among nations of the world, particularly U.S., Great Britain, France, Japan and Italy, a conference was called in Washington by Secretary of State Charles Evans Hughes. It was at this conference that shipbuilding quotas were agreed upon by these naval powers.

The "Ohio gang" led by Harry M. Daugherty was responsible for putting the President in the White House because they felt that he would be easy to manipulate. They proved to be right. Daugherty was able to convince the President to appoint him Attorney General of the United States - a position Daugherty used to solicit payoffs from the bootleggers in exchange for not prosecuting them for violating the eighteenth amendment to the Constitution which prohibited the manufacture, sale, transportation, or consumption of alcoholic beverages in the United States.

There were other scandals which were to greatly discredit the Republican administration of Harding. Charles R. Forbes, head of the newly formed veteran's bureau had difficulty accounting for the disappearance of 200 million dollars. Teapot Dome scandal of the Harding administration is generally ranked as the most serious scandal ever unearthed in the United States. This scandal involved the leasing of government oil reserves to private interests and implicated Albert B. Fall, Secretary of the Interior, as the perpetrator of the illegal transaction. To prevent being ousted from office, Fall turned in his resignation. The President accepted his resignation *with regret*.

President Harding had not been personally involved which characterized his days in office. His only role was in having implicit trust in those of his administration. The President was never accused of being dishonest. The charge of stupidity has arisen on more than one occasion, however. It seems that in their search for a second rater the Republican party came up with a third rater.

While in office Harding moaned repeatedly that the job was too big for him. In one instance while talking to an advisor, Jed Welliver, Harding said: "Jed, I don't know what to do about this taxation issue—there must be some book that could straighten it out in my mind but I don't know where it is and I don't know if I could read it if I found it—maybe there's some college man that could explain it to me but I don't know who he is. My God, but this is a hell of a place for a man like me to be." On one occasion, President Harding's father remarked, "Warren, if you were a girl you'd be in the family way all of the time. You just can't say no."

It was said that the scandals of the Harding administration were so bad that the man in the moon held his nose when he passed over the U.S.

News of the scandals reached Harding as he was on a speaking tour across the United States. He was reportedly devastated by the news. It was on the return trip home that he contracted pneumonia and died. Speculation still persists concerning the cause of the President's death but those close to him felt certain that the disloyalty of trusted friends hastened his death.

When news of Harding's death in 1923 reached Vice President Calvin Coolidge he was visiting at his father's farm in Vermont. He was sworn in as President by his father, a Justice of the Peace, using the old family Bible. Coolidge filled out the unexpired term of Harding and continued the prosperity that the American people were getting quite accustomed to during those post-war years.

The Republicans had no difficulty agreeing to accept President Coolidge as their candidate for the upcoming Presidential election of 1924. The "Golden Twenties" (also remembered as the Jazz Age and the Age of Wonderful Nonsense) were proceeding very nicely: the speakeasies were flourishing with patrons; sports were in their heydays; New Orleans Jazz could be heard throughout the country; the investors were recording record gains at the stock market; and there was always bank night at the local theater. In short, things were very harmonious in the United States giving the Republican party every reason to sense a major victory from a disorganized Democratic party. "Keep cool with Coolidge" was the slogan used very effectively by the Republican party in 1924 to keep the public apprised of the reason for the post-war prosperity.

The race for the Democratic nomination was centered around Alfred E. Smith, Governor of New York, and William McAdoo, son-in-law of former President Wilson and head of the railroad administration during World War I. Unable to agree on either of these two candidates, the convention turned to John W. Davis, a New York corporation lawyer. The Democrats hoped to discredit the Republicans by hanging out the dirty linen of the Harding administration: Teapot Dome, Veteran's Bureau, and prohibition scandals were echoed over and over by Democratic supporters.

Someone once said that corruption in business turns our heads but corruption in government makes us yawn. This certainly had to be true in the election of 1924. Coolidge soundly defeated Davis with 382 electoral votes to Davis' 136.

Somewhat significant in this election which saw two conservatives head to head was the presence of liberal candidate, Robert M. La Follette of Wisconsin who was representing the Socialist party. La Follette did what few third party candidates were unable to do: he broke into the electoral column gaining 13 votes, all from his home state of Wisconsin.

The prosperity of the nation dominated all other considerations during the administration of Calvin Coolidge and it seemed that he should have won the nomination of his party to a second term but this was not to be. While vacationing in the Black Hills of South Dakota Coolidge summoned the press and distributed slips of paper containing the words, "I do not choose to run for President in 1928." There were some who maintained that the President was shocked when the Republican party took him at his word and passed him over for the election of 1928.

Following most wars fought by the United States a military leader emerged as Presidential timber and in many cases elected to the Presidency. World War I was to be an exception to this rule. The leader who appeared out of this recent war was a civilian—Food Administrator Herbert Hoover. The wheatless and meatless days of the "Hooverizing" years were remembered as contributing factors in winning the war. His Belgium relief program was also a big plus.

The Republican party taking Coolidge at his word nominated Herbert C. Hoover, the Secretary of Commerce. "Let's keep what we've got, prosperity just didn't happen," was the popular slogan utilized by the Republicans to take credit for the prosperous times of the period. One of the major planks of the Republican party supported prohibition and bitterly denounced the attempts to repeal the eighteenth amendment to the Constitution.

The only outstanding candidate the Democrats had to consider was four time Governor of New York, Alfred E. Smith. Smith had several things going against him as he maneuvered for the Democratic nomination: He was a Roman Catholic and many felt that the United States was not yet ready for a Catholic President; he was a "wet" and a sizeable portion of the population of the United States felt that "demon rum" was fast becoming the ruination of mankind; he was associated with the corrupt Tammany Society of New York although he was considered to be honest himself. Despite these liabilities Smith was nominated on the first ballot after having been introduced to the convention as the "happy warrior" by Franklin D. Roosevelt. Throughout the campaign, however, Roosevelt remained in the background convinced that the "happy warrior" could not win.

The election results confirmed FDR's fears. Hoover defeated Smith in a landslide 444 electoral votes to 87 for Smith. There were many who attributed Smith's defeat to his religion, but later studies revealed that Smith had done better than Democrat Cox did in 1920 and Democratic candidate Davis did in the election of 1924. While it is true that anti-catholic campaigns were directed against Smith the fact remains that the United States was enjoying an unprecedented era of prosperity and the American voter had no valid reason for making a change in the leadership of the nation. It's quite likely that there wasn't a Democrat alive that could wrest control of the government from the Republican party.

The Bull market continued during the early months of the Hoover administration. Speculators kept investing in the stock market with full confidence that their investments would continue to multiply and reap them huge profits. The exception to this prosperous period were the unorganized work force and farmers who felt that the 1920's were anything but golden.

President Hoover dismissed his "rugged individualism" philosophy by putting his signature to legislation designed to help the farmer out of his blight. The Agricultural Marketing Act created the Federal Farm Board which provided loans to farm organizations. However well intentioned this measure was it fell miserably short of fulfilling its goal.

Somehow it couldn't last. The stock market crash came rather unexpectedly in October, 1929. On "Black Tuesday", October 29, 1929, over sixteen million shares of stock were sold to anyone at almost any price. This crash was to signal the start of the worst depression the nation has ever experienced with many factories forced into bankruptcy and bank failures resulting when they were unable to fill the withdrawal demands of angry depositors.

Selling apples on the street corner became quite commonplace in the United States during this period. A popular song of the time was "Brother, Can You Spare a Dime?"

> Once I built a railroad—made it run
> Made it race against time
> Once I built a railroad—now it's gone
> Brother, can you spare a dime?
>
> Say, don't you remember, you called me Al
> It was Al all the time?
> Say, don't you remember I'm your pal?
> Brother can you spare a dime?

Men wandered aimlessly in search of a job. Unemployed sat in despair, head in their laps on park benches all the day long blaming themselves for not being good providers while deep down they knew that they were innocent victims of the nation's catastrophe. Soup kitchens were set up throughout the United States by charitable organizations to feed the hungry and shanty towns known as "Hoovervilles" were set up by those whose mortgages had been foreclosed on their property. President Hoover insisted that the depression would not last and holding dear to his "rugged individualism" philosophy encouraged charitable organizations to take control until the crisis had passed.

Many reasons have been advanced to explain the causes of the great depression of 1929: overproduction and the accompanying declining prices—manufacturers were producing more products than the people were able to purchase; heavy installment buying—when hard times began to be felt people were unable to continue making their installment payments; uneven distribution of income—a very large percentage of the wealth of the nation was concentrated in the hands of a small percentage of the population; the passage of the Hawley-Smoot tariff of 1930—against the advice of over one thousand leading economists who felt that such a high tariff would lead to reciprocity against American products by other nations as well as to make it virtually impossible for European nations to repay their World War I war debts, President Hoover signed the measure into law. (President Hoover did declare a one year moratorium on the war debts but at the end of the year the European countries liked it so much they decided to continue it indefinitely. Exception: Finland.)

By the time the election of 1932 arrived estimates of the unemployed in this country ran as high as twelve million. The President had started some government programs designed to aid the economic situation—many of them considered to be "New Dealism" in nature but by 1932 the general appraisal of President Hoover's efforts were summed up in the expression, "too little and too late".

President Hoover's statement that the bums were better fed than ever before in our history did not qualify him as a candidate to fear in the upcoming election but the Republican party had to go with the incumbent; to do otherwise would be an admission that

President Hoover was responsible for the economic situation. The Republicans kept telling the people that "prosperity is just around the corner", but all the people were able to see around the corner were deepening bread lines. "A chicken in every pot and two cars in every garage" was a Republican promise being made to the American voter on the eve of the election. A leading cartoonist made a mockery of this promise by sketching a garage with two lonely chickens in it. What many Americans were experiencing was a dismissal slip in every pay envelope.

Worldwide conditions were responsible for the economic chaos found in the United States argued the Republican party. The programs started by Hoover would eventually end the depression if given a chance to work, they asserted. The Republicans proved to be anything but convincing in getting the unemployed to accept another four years of Republican leadership.

The Democratic convention meeting in Chicago felt that their chances of winning their first Presidential election in sixteen years were excellent if they played their cards right. It wasn't in the cards, however, to take another chance with Al Smith and his brown derby, his Catholicism, his New York twang, and his association with the Tammany Society. Smith felt that he certainly deserved another chance for the big house and was extremely disappointed when the convention chose Franklin Delano Roosevelt, a distant cousin of Theodore Roosevelt. Roosevelt had represented the Democratic party in 1920 when he shared the ticket for the Presidency with Cox, he served as Assistant

Secretary of the Navy, and during these depression years served as Governor of New York where he embarked on a huge spending program to relieve the suffering of the unfortunate in that state.

"A new deal for the forgotten man" was the slogan of the Democratic party in 1932. Roosevelt had called for this new deal when he accepted the nomination of his party in Chicago in 1932 and eleven million unemployed felt that he was talking directly to them. In their platform the Democrats called for an end to prohibition, a broad system of public works to aid the unemployed, stricter regulation of the stock market, insurance against bank failures and a balanced budget.

The Republican party platform called for an end to prohibition but less enthusiastically than did the Democrats. They extolled the virtues of the Republican programs enacted to curb the depression and continued to blame the depression on international conditions.

When the returns came in it was a landslide victory for Roosevelt and the Democratic party. Roosevelt carried forty-two states and received 472 electoral votes to Hoover's 59. It was a landslide victory that brought Hoover in and out of the White House. Clearly, the result of this election showed more displeasure over President Hoover's policies than support for the former Governor of New York.

Franklin Roosevelt was not the same person many of his friends remembered him to be in his earlier years. He had been born into wealth and attended the most exclusive schools and ultimately graduated from Harvard. In his earlier years he was considered to be rather arrogant and standoffish. In 1921 infantile paralysis struck Roosevelt resulting in his having to wear steel braces on his legs for the remainder of his life. It was observed that from the time the crippling disease struck Roosevelt he became a different person who showed great compassion for the unfortunate and this compassion would be manifested in his programs designed to end the suffering brought on by the great depression.

From election day, 1932, until March 4, 1933, when Franklin Delano Roosevelt would be sworn in as the thirty-second President of the United States, the American people "held their breath" waiting to see if this miracle man, this man who had promised so much to combat the economic distress of the nation, could deliver on his promises. There was certainly one thing that the American public keenly sensed: he was not afraid. He instilled much confidence in a nation so dreadfully fearful of the future.

In his inaugural address to the nation on March 4, 1933, Franklin Roosevelt reassured all Americans when he stated, "Let me assert my firm belief that the only thing we have to fear is fear itself." He surely felt that the panic that had seized so many Americans had to be put to rest and the confidence in the voice of FDR had the effect of allaying many of these fears.

The Democratic party set right to work. Pouring into Washington, D.C. by the hundreds were recognized experts in practically every field. These experts soon came to be known as the "brain trust" and practically all were graduates of Harvard. The President and his staff did not attend the inaugural ball but set right to work mapping out the programs of the New Deal.

Practically every bill sent to Congress was immediately approved without debate. "The house is on fire—give the President what he needs to put it out," was a popular expression heard on Capitol Hill. In the first hundred days the Democrats pushed through an avalanche of agencies set up to combat the depression.

One of the first acts of President Roosevelt was to declare a "bank holiday". Banks were closed for a period of three days for the purpose of giving the federal government time to supply needed funds to solvent banks. Many "shaky" banks never reopened their doors. In the first of Roosevelt's fireside chats the President urged Americans to take the money from beneath their mattresses and redeposit it in a government approved reopened bank. Confidence in the banking system was restored to many by this act of the federal government.

The New Deal program of the Democratic party consisted of the three "R's": Relief, Recovery, and Reform.

> **Relief**: This was designed to aid the unemployed and would have an immediate effect on those out of work. Some programs found in the relief aspect of the New Deal were:

> **W.P.A.** (Works Progress Administration). The federal government supplied money to the

states to create work for the unemployed. In this program many schools and roads were constructed as well as the construction of government buildings. Artists and writers were employed so as to preserve their skills for post depression years.

C.C.C. (Civilian Conservation Corps). Young men between the ages of eighteen and twenty-five were given the opportunity to attend camps run by the federal government and designed to work on conservation projects. This program had the effect of keeping men of this age off the street corners, out of the already overcrowded labor market, and relieved many families of one more mouth to feed.

N.Y.A. (National Youth Administration). Money was allocated to schools to provide work for students whose father was unemployed. These students would work before and after school hours erasing boards, etc.

F.E.R.A. (Federal Emergency Relief Administration). Those who were on the relief rolls collected money for doing nothing. To qualify they had to be out of work.

H.O.L.C. (Home Owners Loan Corporation). People's homes were saved from foreclosure when the federal government loaned money at a very low interest rate and over a long period of time.

Critics of this aspect of the program vigorously attacked the W.P.A. They maintained that this acronym really stood for "We Poke Along". They maintained that the W.P.A.ers did nothing but lean on their shovels all day long. It seems almost certain that it was they who concocted the story that W.P.A. foremen wrote to Washington asking for a new supply of shovels only to be told that the government was temporarily out of shovels and that the men should lean against the trees until new shovels arrived. These critics charged that the program would not work in the long run. President Roosevelt answered that people did not eat in the long run, they eat every day.

Recovery: This aspect of the program was to bring gradual changes to the economy in the fields of industry, agriculture, labor and commerce. Some programs found in the recovery aspect of the New Deal were:

A.A.A. (Agricultural Adjustment Act). The government paid farmers for restricting production by plowing under a portion of their field. The object was to create a scarcity of these products in an effort to bring prices up. This program was declared unconstitutional by the Supreme Court in the case of U.S. vs. Butler but was immediately replaced with similar measures which met the test of the Supreme Court.

N.R.A. (National Recovery Administration). Codes of fair practices were set down by the government and would be binding on all businesses which became a member. The Blue Eagle emblem was displayed on the store window of each participating business in an effort to stimulate business. Businesses which participated were rewarded with government contracts. This program was designed to last two years but it, too, felt the axe of the Supreme Court. In the case of U.S. vs. Schecter the Supreme Court ruled that this measure was putting legislative power in the hands of the executive branch of the government when it set rules of conduct for business.

P.W.A. (Public Works Administration). The federal government awarded building contracts to industry to stimulate hiring of the unemployed.

N.L.R.A. (National Labor Relations Act). Set up the National Labor Relations Board to arbitrate grievances between labor and management in an effort to avoid strikes.

Reform: This aspect of the new deal was to bring about permanent changes in our economy designed to prevent a recurrence of another depression. Some programs found in the reform aspect of the New Deal were:

F.D.I.C. (Federal Deposit Insurance Corporation). Created by the Glass-Steagall Act, it protected bank deposits in case of bank failures. It was designed to encourage depositors to put their money back into an insured bank.

T.V.A. (Tennessee Valley Authority). Designed to provide inexpensive electricity to people living in the area of the Tennessee River and its tributaries while at the same time act as a recovery measure by providing jobs in the Tennessee Valley area.

S.E.C. (Securities and Exchange Commission). This group would have the responsibility of regulating the stock exchange. They would serve as a watchdog in an effort to protect investors from overvalued and worthless stock.

S.S.A. (Social Security Administration). Designed to provide unemployment insurance, old age pensions, and aid to the unemployables.

Besides the charges of "boondoggling" brought against the W.P.A. there were added charges that the federal government was creating food scarcities at a time when millions of Americans were going to bed hungry. The private power companies criticized the Tennessee Valley Authority and called it undue government intervention into private enterprise and further argued that the federal government was using a 16" yard stick in establishing electrical rates for the Tennessee Valley area. Industry argued that too many benefits had been granted to labor and certainly not least was the cry of legalized robbery from the banking industry when the President devalued the dollar to 59.06 cents in an effort to raise prices. The charges that the President was pushing the country toward bankruptcy fell on deaf ears to those who for the first time in several years walked proudly to their jobs.

The Republican party had reason to fear the outcome of the upcoming election of 1936. Roosevelt, despite mounting criticism, was extremely popular among the masses.

The Republicans decided to stress the mounting debt of the United States brought on by the New Deal program by referring to FDR as Franklin Deficit Roosevelt. In searching for a candidate they turned to Alfred E. Landon, Governor of Kansas. Kansas was the only state in the Union with a balanced budget and so it didn't take the Republicans very long to attach the label "Thrifty Al" to their candidate.

The only question in the minds of the Democrats as the 1936 election approached was the margin by which FDR would win the election. In the campaign the Democrats pointed to the number of people in the work force as compared to the pre-New Deal period. They assailed the Hoover administration and referred to the Republican party as the depression party.

The old saying, "As Maine goes, so goes the Union", didn't prove true in this election of 1936. Roosevelt won forty-six out of the forty-eight states. The two states that went to Landon were Maine and Vermont. It didn't take the exuberant Democrats long to rephrase that old saying to "As Maine goes, so goes Vermont". This election produced the greatest landslide victory since James Monroe ran unopposed in the election of 1820. Al Smith summed up the landslide victory by saying, "No one wanted to shoot Santa Claus.

FDR as he was now affectionately being called took the oath of office on January 20, 1937, instead of the usual March 4 because the twentieth amendment— referred to as the Lame Duck amendment—had been ratified in 1933. This amendment had the effect of shortening the time that a defeated President and defeated Congressmen would remain in office. Defeated Congressmen would leave office January 3.

This landslide victory of Roosevelt was responsible in part for the President to embark upon rather brazen attempts to rid himself of the critics who had opposed his New Deal program. His first attack, much to the amazement of practically everyone was an attack on the Supreme Court of the United States. In addition to the Agricultural Adjustment Act, 1933, and National Recovery Act, 1933, the Supreme Court had declared unconstitutional a number of other New Deal measures which President Roosevelt felt were very necessary to his program. Noting that six of the

Supreme Court justices were over the age of seventy the President came up with a plan which he referred to as "An answer to a maiden's prayer". This plan, the Court Reform Bill, would give the President authority to appoint an additional justice for every justice over the age of seventy who had not retired. This plan would give the President the authority to increase the membership in the Supreme Court to fifteen. "Court packing" was the term used by opponents to this plan to indicate that the President was attempting to get "spineless puppets" in the court that would act as a rubber stamp for anything that the President wanted. A sign that the President was losing some of his popularity showed up when members of his own party in Congress turned down his proposal.

"A switch in time, saves nine", was a popular saying being circulated by those who observed the changing attitude of the Supreme Court toward subsequent New Deal legislation:

> A case concerning minimum wage for women was upheld by the Supreme Court which had the effect of reversing its decision on a similar case the previous year. The Supreme Court also upheld the Wagner Act and the Social Security Act both of which might have run into serious trouble earlier.

Another indication that the President was losing some of his early popularity occurred when the President in one of his many "fireside chats" read off the names of the Congressmen that he wished to have defeated in the 1938 Congressional election. When the election results came in all but one of those on Roosevelt's "hit list" were reelected.

From the time that Germany, under the leadership of Adolph Hitler attacked Poland in 1939 and started World War II, the U.S. had another overriding concern, the fear that the United States might be drawn into the European conflict. Much of the earlier criticism that the President was leading the country into bankruptcy and that the New Deal programs were not ending the depression were now secondary to European conditions and so as the Presidential election of 1940 approached, the focus of attention was to find a way to keep the United States out of World War II.

Things were "looking up' for the Third Reich as the election of 1940 made its appearance. France had already fallen and the only obstacle left in the way of total conquest of Europe by the Nazis was Great Britain. The interventionists and the isolationists within the United States were standing toe to toe. The isolationists led by former hero, Charles A. Lindberg maintained that the United States defenses be bolstered but that the U.S. should stay out of the war. The interventionists argued that the U.S. should give Great Britain any aid, including troops, for the impending Battle of Britain which the British were preparing for. They agreed completely with Winston Churchill, now Prime Minister of Great Britain, that if Hitler was not stopped the whole world, including the United States would sink into the abyss of a new dark age.

No one was more in tune with the necessity for some kind of aid for Great Britain in meeting Hitler's challenge than President Roosevelt. The German U-boats were very successful in their attacks on shipping and the British were in desperate need of destroyers to combat the U-boat menace. In an effort to aid the British the President assigned fifty "overage destroyers" to Britain in exchange for bases in the Atlantic. This action of the President which came to be known as The Destroyer Deal did not set well with the isolationists but neither were they ecstatic about the first peacetime draft in U.S. history enacted in 1940 nor the two ocean navy proposed by the President in preparation for a possible confrontation with the Japanese.

The nominating conventions of 1940 posed serious problems for both the Republicans and the Democrats. The Republican front runners appeared to be Senator Robert A. Taft of Ohio, son of former President William Howard Taft, and Thomas E. Dewey of New York but a newcomer to politics, Wendell L. Willkie, an interventionist of German descent stole the limelight and won the nomination of the Republican party. The Democrats, on the other hand, were in a very confused state. No President had ever broken the two term tradition inaugurated by George Washington. Despite the early statement of Roosevelt that he longed for retirement there was still the expectation that the President might change his mind and decide to run for a third term. The Democratic convention kept "spinning its wheels" waiting for some word from the President of his true intentions. Finally, Roosevelt announced that he would not turn his back on America in this time of crisis - he would seek a third term. He won the nomination on the first ballot.

The campaign of 1940 tossed about the New Deal gains and failures. Willkie, a former Democrat and liberal didn't disagree with the New Deal programs per se but felt that he could carry them out more efficiently and economically. The Democrats of course stressed the successes of the program and emulating the typical political party ignored the shortcomings. Both parties, however, knew that the chief concern of the electorate centered around the chances of American boys fighting on distant lands and expectedly both parties promised that the United States would keep out of the foreign war unless attacked. The Republicans, not at all surprisingly, called for a constitutional amendment limiting a President to two terms while the Democrats proclaimed that "Two good terms deserve a third".

Franklin Delano Roosevelt was elected to an unprecedented third term defeating Wendell Willkie who ran a close race. In an election that had more people turning out at the polls than in any previous Presidential election Roosevelt won in the popular vote by five million votes. The result was much closer than the electoral vote 449-82 would indicate. This election also had the Republicans gaining seats in the Senate and in the House of Representatives although the Democrats continued to control both houses.

The American policy of "cash and carry" in regard to the purchase of war materials which was an integral part of the U.S. neutrality laws while greatly favoring the allied nations at the outset was now becoming a liability to the allied cause. Great Britain was now experiencing great difficulty in raising the necessary cash for the purchases. To overcome this obstacle Roosevelt, with the support of Congress instituted the Lend Lease Program in 1941. This act made America "the arsenal of democracy" by selling, transferring, leasing or lending war materials to any country whose defense was deemed vital to the defense of the United States. The United States was not so neutral any more.

President Roosevelt was not quite a year into his third term when he became a wartime President. On December 7, 1941, the Japanese launched an attack on the American base at Pearl Harbor on the Hawaiian Island of Oahu and also struck at other U.S. Pacific bases. The President immediately summoned Congress to declare that a state of war exists between the United States and the Empire of Japan. In his message President Roosevelt referred to Sunday, December 7, 1941, as "a day which shall live in infamy". It has.

For the remainder of the President's term there was no matter more pressing than to gear the United States for the wartime emergency and to do all that would hasten the final victory and bring our American boys home to their families once again. A return to normalcy never meant more than it did following our entrance into World War II.

By 1944 the war was winding down; it seemed only a matter of time that the war would be finished in Europe. Back home it was business as usual on the political scene; there was a Presidential election to be held. Meeting in Chicago, the Republicans nominated Thomas E. Dewey, Governor of New York. The Democrats also meeting in Chicago nominated

Franklin Delano Roosevelt to a fourth term by acclamation. Roosevelt's health was failing and so the Democrats put special emphasis on their selection of a Vice Presidential candidate. The incumbent Vice President Henry A. Wallace would like to have continued in that capacity but there were enough delegate votes opposing his nomination to get Harry S. Truman of Missouri named.

The campaign of 1944 was a difficult one for the Republicans. They would dare not challenge the Democratic strategies used in fighting the war—that indeed would be extremely unpatriotic at a time when patriotism had hit an all time high in the United States. They chose instead to attack the "old men" in Washington and urged for a change. President Roosevelt, busy with the war effort, did not do much campaigning in the early days of the campaign but toward the closing days he "took to the stump".

A war-weary America didn't have very much to laugh about during these war days, but President Roosevelt did manage to get them to smile a bit with his famous Fala speech. Roosevelt had been accused by the Republicans of leaving his Scotty dog, Fala, on an Aleutian Island and sending a destroyer back to fetch him at a tremendous cost in dollars to the American public. In alluding to this charge President Roosevelt told the American public in one of his fireside chats that when his dog, Fala, heard of these charges her Scottish soul was furious and she hasn't been the same dog since. It proved to be a welcomed diversion.

Roosevelt was elected to a fourth term defeating Dewey 432-99 in the electoral vote. The Democratic slogan, "a poor time to swap horses" seemed to make a lot of sense to the electorate. After all, the war was going good for the allies and it doesn't make a whole lot of sense to swap horses in the middle of the stream.

The war was all but over in Europe when the President was inaugurated to his fourth term. The Germans would surrender May 7, 1945, to the allied armies but FDR would not be around to rejoice in it. A shocked world would be informed on April 12, 1945, that President Roosevelt succumbed to a massive cerebral hemorrhage at Warm Springs, Georgia. Always before, the President found relief from his trips to Warm Springs but the strain of twelve years in the White House during very troubled times had finally taken its toll.

Vice President Truman upon assuming the Presidency asked the reporters gathered there for their prayers. He knew that there was still a war in the Pacific to be won and that extremely difficult decisions would have to be made by him in the years ahead.

No President of the United States has ever been confronted with a decision the magnitude of that which President Truman was required to make. The United States had developed the atomic bomb and if used against the Japanese it would avoid an invasion of Japan by the United States, an invasion that undoubtedly would result in the loss of thousands of lives of American servicemen.

The President was acutely aware of the vast destruction and tremendous loss of life the use of the bomb would exact, but American lives could be saved by its use and this was paramount to the President. He authorized the use of the bomb on the cities of Hiroshima and Nagasaki. Within days the Japanese surrendered to the United States and World War II would become history.

During Truman's administration Russia, our former ally of World War II, in violation of the Atlantic Charter and the Yalta Conference pulled an "Iron Curtain" over her weak neighbors. To confront Russia and attempt to contain communism the President adopted a policy which became known as the Truman Doctrine. This doctrine appropriated U.S. dollars to Greece and Turkey in an effort to enable these countries to ward off a communistic takeover. Greece and Turkey were not the only countries of Europe in dire need of American Dollars to achieve the same objective. To enlarge on the aid given to Greece and Turkey the United States adopted what came to be known as the European Recovery Program or Marshall Plan (named after General George C. Marshall). This program had the effect of appropriating billions of dollars to the European Nations that cooperated in a plan to help themselves rise up economically. The Marshall plan proved to be a great success; European countries would, in the program, become economically independent quicker than expected. From this point forward, however, the United States and the Soviet Union would become engaged in a "Cold War". The U.S. Policy of containment would be diametrically opposed to the Russian goal of spreading Communism throughout the world.

On the domestic scene the Taft Hartley Act, a measure passed over the veto of President Truman, was pushed through by the Republicans in an effort to take back some of the gains made by organized labor during the New Deal period. Also a Presidential succession act was passed which altered the order in which the office of the Presidency would be filled in case of the death of the President. This new measure provided that the Speaker of the House and the President of the Senate in that order would assume the high office upon the death of the President and the Vice President. They would be followed by cabinet members in order of creation. Prior to this change the cabinet members followed the Vice President. This change made the government more responsive to the people since the Speaker of the House and President of the Senate are elected officials.

There weren't a whole lot of people who thought that President Truman had a chance to be elected in his own right in 1948. At the Democratic Convention held in Philadelphia the delegates chose Truman after General Eisenhower did not respond to their flirtations. There was disunity at this Democratic Convention particularly in the South where Truman's Civil Rights stand alienated many of his early supporters. Angrily, some Southern Democrats calling themselves "Dixiecrats" organized the States Rights Party at their own convention held in Birmingham, Alabama and nominated Strom Thurmond, Governor of South Carolina as their candidate. Vice President Henry Wallace split the party even further by running for President on the new Progressive Party.

The Republican Party had sufficient reason to feel confident of victory for the forthcoming election of 1948: they had won the Congressional elections of 1946; they felt that sixteen years of Democratic rule would be all that the voters could tolerate; the Democratic Party was split three ways; and in their eyes the fact that President Truman was the first since Cleveland who did not have a college degree was becoming more and more apparent. Confidently they once again nominated Governor Thomas E. Dewey of New York.

Quite possibly the only person in the United States predicting a victory for President Truman in the 1948 election was President Truman. At one point he called a press conference at which he said, "You boys are probably wondering who the next President will be— well you're looking at him." All the leading polls were predicting that the President hadn't much of a chance in the election and so, too, were the leading newspapers in the country—especially the Chicago Tribune which ran off an early edition with the following headline, "DEWEY DEFEATS TRUMAN".

In the biggest upset of any U.S. Presidential election ever held President Truman defeated Dewey 303-189. The popular vote favored Truman by over two million votes, and yet he became a minority President. It didn't take Truman long, however, to have his picture taken holding a copy of the Chicago Tribune aloft with those blazing headlines clearly visible.

In analyzing the outcome of this election it is felt that overconfidence among the Republicans had to be considered a major cause of the upset. Other factors which brought this unexpected result were the Black voters who liked the civil rights plank of the Democratic party, organized labor disliked the Taft-Hartley Act and many Americans who liked "gutsy" Harry.

President Truman gave the name Fair Deal to his program. This program was essentially a continuation of many New Deal Programs and which was accused by the Republicans of out Roosevelting Roosevelt by creating a welfare state.

The Cold War turned into a Hot War on June 25, 1950 when the Communist North Korean Army - Russian trained and Russian equipped invaded South Korea by crossing below the 38 degree parallel separating North and South Korea. This invasion had the effect of Russia throwing a direct challenge at the U.N., (World War II's answer to the League of Nations). The U.N. met the challenge head on when the security council, taking advantage of Russia's absence, (Russia was boycotting the U.N. because Communist China was denied admittance), branded North Korea the aggressor and called on all nations to stop the North Korean aggression.

The Korean War was still in progress when the election of 1952 approached. The Republicans, with the 1948 upset still fresh in their minds, were cautiously optimistic. Robert A. Taft was being pushed by many for the nomination of the Republican Party but acknowledging that the Taft-Hartley Act, 1947, would cost many votes to Taft the Republicans looked elsewhere for a candidate. Their search ended when in

January, 1952, Dwight David Eisenhower announced that he was a Republican and would accept the nomination of the Republican Party if offered to him. The "I Like Ike" buttons were being manufactured by the millions to be available for the Chicago Republican Convention.

Supporters of Taft stepped aside and permitted Eisenhower to be nominated on the first ballot. As his running mate Eisenhower chose Richard M. Nixon.

The twenty-second amendment was added to the Constitution during Truman's administration and had the effect of limiting a President's tenure in office to ten years. This amendment was pushed along by the Republicans obviously because of four term Roosevelt. This amendment was not to apply to the President in office at the time of its ratification and therefore was not applicable to President Truman. This, however, became academic when Truman decided not to seek reelection.

The Democrats in seeking a candidate settled for Adlai Stevenson, Governor of Illinois, who unfortunately was not very well known outside his own State of Illinois.

The campaign of 1952 was hard fought. The Republicans attacked the corruption of the Truman administration, (the mink dynasty), and promised to clean up "the mess in Washington". There probably wasn't a more admired man in America than "Ike" who had been the Supreme Commander of the Allied Forces in Europe during World War II and when he made the statement that if it took a personal trip to

Korea to end the war, "I shall make that trip; I shall go to Korea," he was a shoe-in to defeat Stevenson.

The Democrats knew that they had a formidable adversary in Eisenhower. They felt that their best weapon was the Hoover depression and so they played up the prosperity enjoyed in America under Democratic Administrations.

It was a landslide victory and this time it was the Republican Party that rejoiced in it. Eisenhower captured 442 electoral votes to Stevenson's 89.

One interesting consequence of this election was the capturing of four Southern States by the Republican Party. Tennessee, Virginia, Florida, and Texas served notice on the Democratic Party that the South was no longer "Solid". The Southern States would no longer be taken for granted by the Democratic Party.

President Eisenhower ushered in what was to be referred to as "Modern Republicanism". Eisenhower was to continue some of the New Deal and Fair Deal Programs of Roosevelt and Truman rather than scrap all programs attributed to Democratic predecessors.

Somewhat disappointing to the Republican Party was the slim majority by which they won Congress in 1952 despite the landslide victory of Eisenhower. They were to be bitterly disappointed in the 1954 congressional elections when the Democrats were successful in winning control of both houses of Congress. Some Republicans wondered if it was only Ike that the people liked among the Republicans.

There was great concern in the Republican camp about the chances of President Eisenhower again becoming their candidate for President in 1956. He had suffered a heart attack and the feeling among many was that he could not endure a grueling campaign. Eisenhower's physicians, however, gave him a clean bill of health. The Republicans then renominated Eisenhower and Nixon to represent their ticket.

The Democrats again chose Adlai Stevenson and selected Estes Kefauver of Tennessee as his running mate.

During the campaign the Republicans stressed the prosperity the nation was enjoying while the Democrats took a slap at the high prices the consumer was being forced to pay and pointed to the distress of the farmer.

Once again it was an Eisenhower landslide winning 457 electoral votes to Stevenson's 73. It was a different story in the Congressional races. The Democrats increased their control of Congress by substantial margins. In the Congressional election of 1958 the Democrats won both houses in a landslide and so President Eisenhower was forced to work with a Democratic Congress during his entire second administration.

During the Eisenhower years the Cold War was to occupy much of the President's time and concern. The Korean War was brought to a halt in 1953 but the problems of concern to the United States were the revolt in Poland in 1956, The Hungarian Revolt in 1956, and the Suez Crisis. Further alarming to the U.S. was the shooting down of a U-2 plane by the Russians on the eve of the Summit Conference scheduled between the U.S. and Russia. Trouble in the Mid East and Far East further aggravated world peace and America's pride was shattered when the Russians launched Sputnik. Such were the situations confronting the U.S. as the election of 1960 approached.

The Republican Party would like to have renominated Eisenhower to a third term in 1960 but this was not to be. The Twenty-second Amendment which they had pushed so hard to get ratified was to come back to haunt them. Instead they nominated Richard M. Nixon who had served as Vice President during the Eisenhower administration. On the ticket with Nixon was U.S. Ambassador to the United Nations Henry Cabot Lodge, Jr.

The Democrats hoping to unseat the Republicans in the Presidential race of 1960 went out on a limb and selected John F. Kennedy who, if elected, would become the youngest elected President in U.S. history. John F. Kennedy was a Roman Catholic and this was sure to invoke many inquiries from those who wondered whether his religious convictions would stand in the way of Administering his office. To share the ticket with Kennedy the Democrats chose Lyndon Johnson of Texas who had been a member of Congress for twenty-three years and was at the time the Senate Majority leader.

The chief issue during the campaign was the Cold War. The Kennedy camp charged that the Russians were advancing Communism throughout the world at a rapid pace while Nixon maintained that under the Eisenhower administration the Communists had been substantially contained.

Highlighting this election was a series of four televised debates between Kennedy and Nixon. Kennedy promised that if elected he would march the U.S. to a "New Frontier."

There was and still is considerable disagreement concerning the outcome of the debates. Kennedy was to present himself as a knowledgeable "youngster". He seemed to be right on top of the critical issues facing the country and showed himself to be anything but the immature lad of forty-three depicted by the elderly forty-seven year old Nixon. In one respect it appears that Kennedy got the better of the debates in that the virtually unknown Senator from Massachusetts was now as popularly known to the American voter as the former Vice President of the United States.

In one of the closest elections in the history of the United States Kennedy was to eke out a victory defeating Nixon 303-219 in electoral votes and winning the popular vote by a scant 118,000 votes out of 68,000,000 cast. He would therefore start his administration as a minority President with the knowledge that there was little endorsement of his new frontier during the recent election. Significant in the outcome of the election were that Kennedy at the age of forty-three would become the youngest elected President of the United States and that he would become the first Catholic elected to the Presidency.

One of Kennedy's first programs was the creation of the Peace Corp. This program attracted young men and women who went to backward countries to aid them in their recovery. Less successful was a program to aid Latin American Countries. The Alliance for Progress fell short of its goals.

The low water mark of the Kennedy administration came to be known as the Bay of Pigs. When the President took office he learned of a plan conceived during the Eisenhower administration whereby Cuban exiles would invade Cuba with the sole purpose of overthrowing Fidel Castro who, with aid from the Russians, was getting stronger every day. President Kennedy went along with the plan with one notable exception - the United States would not become directly involved. The ensuing invasion of Cuba by the Cuban exiles turned out to be a fiasco; they were soundly beaten by Castro forces and forced to surrender. The U.S. failure to intervene had proved costly to the invaders. President Kennedy won applause from many Americans when he took full responsibility for the blunders though many knew that he could have directed the blame elsewhere. To "rescue" the Cuban exiles held captive by the Castro regime the President arranged through private contributions to ransom them back by supplying drugs and heavy industrial equipment to Cuba.

The high water mark of the Kennedy administration occurred when observation planes of the U.S. detected missile sights in Cuba capable of destroying American cities. It was obvious to the U.S. that these sites were the work of the Russians. President Kennedy won high praise when he directed that a quarantine of all offensive weapons to Cuba was in effect. A confrontation of U.S. Naval vessels with Russian ships caused a great deal of consternation both in the U.S. and the Soviet Union but President Kennedy had no intention of backing down. Each day the Russian vessels bound for Cuba continued on their way and the tensions were reaching a critical point. Such tensions were manifested in the nation's schools when the school children with the aid of their parents were to map out the most direct route home in case of any emergency. "Red Alerts" became common in schools throughout the country when, upon signal, school children were directed to seek shelter in designated areas.

Premier Khrushchev at the last minute instructed the approaching Russian vessels to return home and thus prevented a confrontation with the United States Navy whose instructions were clearly understood. A face-saving feature for Khrushchev was America's promise not to invade Cuba if Russia would remove the missile sights from Cuba.

A sign of the popularity of President Kennedy's resolve was shown in the Congressional elections of 1962 when the Democrats made gains in both the House and the Senate. (It is usually customary for the party in power to lose ground in the mid-term elections.)

One of the last acts of President Kennedy was to successfully negotiate a nuclear test ban agreement with Russia. This measure had the effect of restricting nuclear tests in the atmosphere, under water, and in space. This measure was signed by the United States, Great Britain, and Russia.

President Kennedy proved to be a very popular President; he brought great charisma to the high office.

He wasn't to achieve all of the goals he set for himself because his tenure was cut short on November 22, 1963, when he fell victim to an assassin's bullets while riding in a motorcade in downtown Dallas.

There was hardly a dry eye in the United States for the following three days as the American public viewed the television coverage of the ceremonies leading up to the burial of President Kennedy in the Arlington National Cemetery. The reaction of the nation to the assassination of JFK was manifested in the number of schools, highways, airfields, etc., that were renamed after a President who had won the love and admiration of countless millions both at home and abroad.

Vice President Lyndon Baines Johnson having been sworn in as our thirty-sixth President of the United States vowed to continue the fight for legislation that President Kennedy had fought so hard to achieve: civil rights legislation, war on poverty, and a tax cut. Before Congress adjourned in 1964 a civil rights act was passed and the Office of Economic Opportunity was created to provide funds to fight the war on poverty.

An interesting election took place in 1964, the election that President Kennedy had anxiously awaited. This election would pit an ultra-conservative Republican, Barry Goldwater, Senator from Arizona against a liberal Democratic candidate. President Kennedy had looked forward to this election so that the issue of whether this country was conservative or liberal could be put to rest once and for all. With the death of JFK it was now incumbent upon President Johnson to settle the issue.

During the campaign it became necessary for the Republicans to urge the press to print what Goldwater meant and not what he said. At one point in the campaigning Goldwater had suggested the use of atomic bombs to bring the Viet Nam War to an end. It didn't take the Democrats long to have bumper stickers printed which read, "HELP BARRY STAMP OUT PEACE".

It's interesting that in this Presidential election the candidate representing the party of Abraham Lincoln was urging segregation of the races while a Southerner fought for integration. Because of this situation Goldwater was to lose most of the Black vote while Johnson lost some support from fellow Southerners who felt betrayed.

The outcome of the election was a landslide victory for the Democratic party. Goldwater was able to acquire a mere fifty-two electoral votes against 486 for Johnson and recording only twenty-six million votes while Johnson gathered forty-two million. Congress also saw Democratic majorities being voted in.

The Great Society was Johnson's plan for improving the conditions which would enable all Americans to enjoy a higher standard of living. Measures passed during Johnson's administration which put him closer to realizing this dream were Medicare, a program of health insurance for the elderly; greater appropriations for the office of economic opportunity; greater Federal aid to education; and improvement of housing.

The Viet Nam War was escalating and so was the impatience of the Americans who felt that President Johnson was not doing enough to bring the war to an end. Those who supported the war were known as "Hawks" and those who opposed it were called "Doves". America had always entered a war with great resolve, got the job done satisfactorily and brought the servicemen back to a hero's welcome. This was not happening in the Viet Nam War and even members of the President's own party were openly critical of his handling of the war.

It was Eugene J. McCarthy, a leading "Dove", who led a challenge to Johnson's nomination by the Democrats for the 1968 Presidential election by entering and winning the New Hampshire primary. Shortly following McCarthy's New Hampshire victory, Robert F. Kennedy, brother of slain John F. Kennedy, announced that he, too, would oppose Johnson for the nomination of the Democratic Party in 1968.

President Johnson stunned the nation when he announced over television that he would not be a candidate for nomination of his party for 1968. This announcement opened the door for Vice President Humphrey, a "Hawk" who supported Johnson's war policies, to become the third Democratic candidate to enter the race for the upcoming Presidential election.

A tragedy occurred in June, 1968, when Robert Kennedy was assassinated shortly after winning the California primary in a close battle with Eugene McCarthy. It was at a Los Angeles Hotel where the assassin, Sirhan Sirhan, ended the life of Robert F.

Kennedy. The previous April the nation had been shocked over the assassination of the great civil rights leader, Dr. Martin Luther King, the recipient of the Nobel Peace Prize in 1964, and now with the assassination of RFK many Americans began to wonder if it was not becoming fashionable in the United States to snuff out the lives of leaders with whom we disagreed.

Richard M. Nixon who had lost the Presidential race of 1960 to John F. Kennedy and later lost the gubernatorial race of California must have felt that his political aspirations were at an end when he inquired of the reporters, "Now that Nixon's gone who are you guys going to kick around?" Nothing could have been farther from the truth; he was to become the candidate of the Republican Party for the Presidency in 1968. During his "retirement" from politics in 1962 Nixon had devoted all of his energies toward supporting Republican candidates throughout the Nation and his party showed its appreciation for his efforts with this nomination.

The Democrats met in Chicago in 1968 to nominate their candidate and what the American public witnessed on their television screens proved to be one of the most disgraceful sights ever witnessed by a television audience. The hippies and the yippies, opponents of the Viet Nam War, converged on Chicago to manifest their displeasure with the Democratic Party over the war issue. The Chicago police were captured on camera beating the dissenters with their clubs and within moments the cameras were directed inside the convention hall to Chicago Mayor

Daley who appeared unconcerned over the happenings outside the hall. The Chicago police argued later that they were merely reacting to the action of the hippies and yippies that were not recorded by the television cameramen.

All of the efforts of the McCarthy and Kennedy forces to prevent Hubert Humphrey from receiving the nomination fell short when he was nominated on the first ballot. As his running mate, Humphrey chose Edward S. Muskie of Maine.

A third party candidate, George C. Wallace, an extreme Hawk, representing the American Independent Party entered the race.

The big issues in this election were law and order, the Vietnamese War, and Racial unrest. Each of the candidates had "fool-proof" panaceas for correcting all of those inadequacies. Nixon maintained that he had a secret plan to bring the War to an end.

The election result was close, indeed. Nixon won the election but he won by only 260,000 votes out of 71,000,000 votes cast. In the electoral vote tally Nixon had garnered 302, Humphrey had gained 191, and Wallace received 45. Spiro T. Agnew of Maryland became the new Vice President.

As President Nixon continued his efforts to bring the Vietnam War to its conclusion, the Paris Peace Talks were progressing but not as rapidly as he wished. He was constantly reminded of the statement he made during the campaign of 1968 that if he couldn't bring the war to an end in four years he didn't deserve to be reelected. On January 27, 1970 the United States, North Vietnam, South Vietnam, and the Viet Cong signed a peace agreement. The nation's longest and most unpopular war was now over. The Vietnam Soldiers would now return home to unenthusiastic "home folks".

John F. Kennedy had promised a man on the moon by 1970. Had he lived he would have been as delighted and proud as the rest of America when Americans set foot on the moon in 1969. Neil A. Armstrong became the first human to touch down on the moon and as he did he remarked, "That's one small step for a man, one giant leap for mankind."

The twenty-sixth amendment to the Constitution was ratified in 1971 giving eighteen year olds the right to vote and so these young men and women could now look forward with new meaning to the upcoming election of 1972.

A change in the U.S. policy toward the People's Republic of China occurred in 1972 when President Nixon, taking advantage of the rift that developed between Russia and mainland China visited that Nation. As a result of that visit diplomatic relations between the two nations began.

The Soviet Union saw a need to relieve tensions existing between the U.S. and U.S.S.R. and they welcomed President Nixon to their country in 1972. Nixon's visit would mark the first time an American President had visited the Soviet Union since World War II and it ushered in a period of detente between the U.S.A. and the U.S.S.R. An important step toward peace was taken when the SALT, (Strategic Arms Limitation Talks), agreement was signed which limited the types and numbers of military warheads and missiles that each country could deploy.

The Republican Party confidently renominated Nixon for the 1972 election. It appeared almost certain that Nixon would be swept into the Presidency for a second term. His visits to China and Soviet Union were extremely popular; the economy was stable; and prior to the election the announcement was made of a breakthrough in the Paris Peace talks.

Many Democrats were not very enthusiastic over the choice of Senator George McGovern of South Dakota. He was felt by many to be too liberal in his thinking. McGovern's chances were diminished when it was discovered that his running mate Senator Thomas Eagleton of Missouri had a history of mental illness. Concern mounted over Eagleton's qualifications and McGovern was to replace him with Sargent Shriver, brother-in-law of John F. and Robert F. Kennedy.

During the campaign in dovelike manner McGovern argued against the Vietnam War but the Vietnam War was fast becoming a dead issue with the peace talks progressing so smoothly. Nixon, on the other hand took credit for the economy and made sure that the American public was aware that the Vietnam War was practically over.

Nixon won in a landslide. The only state that he was unable to carry was Massachusetts. He received close to sixty-one per cent of the popular vote and in the electoral vote he edged out McGovern 521-17. Spiro Agnew of Maryland was to continue as Vice President.

President Nixon and Vice President Agnew had high expectations of going down in history as a team whose great strides in domestic and foreign affairs would earn them a prominent place in history. They had hoped that their administration could serve as a role model for later chief executives to imitate.

As it turned out the Nixon-Agnew team would go down in history but not as a role model for subsequent administrations. They would earn the inimitable honor of bringing to shame the high offices of President and Vice President. The only honor the history books would reserve for them would be that of being the only President and Vice President to resign their high offices in disgrace.

Vice President Agnew resigned the Vice Presidency when it was revealed that as Governor of Maryland he had accepted kickbacks from contractors and it was alleged that he had continued to receive them after he entered the White House. Nixon, on the other hand was shown to have been involved in the break-in at the Democratic headquarters at the Watergate Complex during the campaigning for the election of 1972.

The whole sordid story of the Watergate break-in had broken during the campaigning for the election but the voting public seemed unconcerned about it after President Nixon announced that White House counsel John Dean had investigated the incident and found that no one in the White House staff was involved in the "very bizarre situation". The Watergate story began when the committee to elect the President, (CREEP), headed by former Attorney General John Mitchell hired "burglars" to break into the Democratic headquarters in the Watergate apartment complex in Washington, D.C. These burglars were arrested by Washington, D.C. police. During the investigation by the police it was revealed that these men were no ordinary burglars. James McCord one of those arrested was a former CIA agent and an address book carried by another burglar contained the name of another CIA agent, E. Howard Hunt. It was beginning to seem there must have been some direct connection with the White House.

The FBI entered the case and prosecuted those directly involved in the burglary plus E. Howard Hunt and G. Gordon Liddy, a lawyer for CREEP. The presiding Judge, John Sirica, sentenced these men to prison terms and also produced a letter from McCord which threw light on the probability that the White House was involved in the incident. Two Washington Post reporters Carl Bernstein and Bob Woodward added credence to this probability when they revealed that one of the burglars had a checking account in the amount of $89,000 acquired from CREEP.

President Nixon accepted the resignation of H.R. Haldeman and John Erlichman his two closest personal aides when it was found that they had been instrumental in covering up the incident. Much pressure was now being brought to bear on the investigation to see what part if any the President had played in the burglary.

To this end a special committee was set up by the Senate and headed by Senator Sam Ervin of North Carolina. The committee hearings were televised for three months and forced the soap operas to take a back seat while the American public had adopted new matinee idols.

During the course of the hearings it was revealed that John Mitchell then Attorney General was present when the plans for Watergate were formulated. By far the most incriminating information came from John Dean who testified that President Nixon continued to suppress information concerning the burglary and indeed authorized payment for bribes to the burglars to keep them from talking.

When news that tape recordings were routinely made of all conversations with the President, efforts to retrieve these tapes went into high gear. Archibald Cox, a special Watergate prosecutor appointed by Nixon's new Attorney General Elliott Richardson, demanded that the tapes be turned over to the investigating commission. President Nixon refused claiming "executive privilege" for the sake of national security and ordered his Attorney General to fire Cox.

Elliott Richardson refused to fire Cox and promptly resigned. Nixon's Solicitor General fired Cox followed by a storm of bills introduced into the House calling for the impeachment of President Nixon.

The House Judiciary Committee began deliberation on the impeachment of the President.

The President under severe pressure appointed a new special prosecutor and released the tapes to Judge Sirica. It was revealed, however, that some of the tapes were missing and on a very crucial tape there was an eighteen and a half minute segment which had been erased. The erasure was felt to have been done deliberately.

The new special prosecutor, Ron Jaworski of Texas, demanded the rest of the tapes from President Nixon. Nixon submitted edited tapes which proved to be unsatisfactory to both Jaworski and the Judiciary Committee. Jaworski then obtained an order from Judge Sirica demanding that the President turn over the tapes. Nixon appealed to the Supreme Court which upheld Sirica's order.

The Judiciary Committee passed three articles of impeachment against President Nixon. This action then persuaded the President to turn over the rest of the tapes - tapes which indisputably showed that the President had known of the burglary and had hindered the investigation by the FBI.

The President's staunchest supporters now started to desert him like fleas leave a dying dog. On August 8, 1974, President Nixon appeared on National television to announce his resignation. Gerald R. Ford who had been selected by President Nixon upon the resignation of Spiro Agnew then became President.

President Ford was a welcomed relief to the high office of the Presidency. His promise of "openness and candor" proved to be extremely well received. He was known to be extremely honest and hard working and brought to the White House a down to earth lifestyle. The President taking advantage of the twenty-fifth amendment to the Constitution appointed Nelson Rockefeller as his Vice President. (Nixon had also utilized the twenty-fifth amendment in appointing

Gerald R. Ford Vice President following the resignation of Spiro Agnew.)

Gerald R. Ford was well liked by most Americans but his pardoning powers got in the way of a lasting friendship. Using the rationale that he wanted to spare the nation the ordeal of having a former President put on trial, Ford pardoned Nixon for any crimes he might have committed while in office. Polls showed that the majority of Americans disagreed that Nixon should be immune to prosecution. There are still many who feel that a deal was made between Nixon and Ford—a second "corrupt bargain" charge.

Most Americans were equally upset by Ford's pardoning (amnesty), to those who had illegally avoided military service during the Vietnam War. Service groups joined by other Star Spangled Banner Americans felt that this action on the part of President Ford was reprehensible. As it turned out, however, few people took advantage of the offer for alternative national service.

The scorecard of President Ford did show that he helped America forget the bitter days of Watergate and once again brought renewed respect for the Presidency. On July 4, 1976, enthusiastic flag waving Americans gleefully celebrated America's bicentennial.

As the 1976 election approached President Ford had to fight off a challenge from former Governor of California, Ronald Reagan, who was being supported by the conservative wing of the Republican Party. In a hard fought contest Ford won a narrow victory.

The Democrats put their hopes on the former Governor of Georgia, Jimmy Carter. He had stunned many by winning primary after primary and this was to render him the only logical Democratic candidate to oppose incumbent Ford.

During the campaign Jimmy Carter, in a slap at former President Nixon and in an effort to refresh the people's memory of Watergate, promised "I will never lie to you." The high cost of living, the problems of unemployment and energy crisis were the primary concerns during the campaigning.

Carter was to defeat Ford by the electoral count of 297-241 in a very close election. He was to receive less than two million more popular votes than Ford. It appeared obvious that the strong civil rights record of Carter as Governor of Georgia made him popular with the black voters. Organized labor saw Jimmy Carter as an ally and lent their support to him also.

When Carter decided that he would make the run for the Presidency there weren't many people who felt that this Georgia Governor who had extremely limited experience in National and International politics had much of a chance of even receiving the nomination of the Democratic Party. One of the first persons he told of his decision to run for President was his mother and when he informed her of his decision her reply was, "President of what, Jimmy?"

President Carter had deep religious convictions and this proved to be very refreshing coming on the heels of the Watergate mess. Like Truman, President Carter was rather folksy and made the average person feel that he was one of them. He was to describe this style as "a southern peanut farmer populist type".

During his administration President Carter experienced much difficulty with Congress in getting many of his pet measures put into practice mainly because he did not have any close ties with Congress. Not having had any previous personal experience in the House or the Senate he was looked upon as an "outsider". He desperately tried to bring about needed tax reform in an effort to remove the loopholes that were permitting millionaires to avoid paying income taxes. The measure that finally came out of Congress did little to alleviate the loopholes that favored the rich.

In foreign affairs President Carter put a high priority on human rights. Unfortunately some of our closest allies were guilty of violating human rights and in these cases the President found it necessary to soft pedal his attacks on them while those nations less of an ally of the United States found guilty were treated more harshly.

Another issue that caused heated debate within the United States centered around the Panama Canal Treaty. President Carter in an effort to have Latin American Countries see the U.S. in a better light agreed to a series of Treaties granting Panama control of the Canal Zone by the year 2000.

The highlight of the Carter administration was the Summit Meeting between President Anwar Sadat of Egypt and Prime Minister Begin of Israel held at Camp David in Maryland. Sadat had visited Israel in 1977 and with Begin agreed to work out a peaceful solution to their differences. Their attempts at agreement ended in disagreements over many basic issues and when it

123

appeared that their movement was about to collapse President Carter invited both gentlemen to visit the United States to continue the deliberations. At the conclusion of the twelve day meeting the "Framework for Peace in the Middle East" was signed by both leaders which paved the way for a peace treaty between Egypt and Israel which returned the Sinai territory to Egypt.

In an effort to bring about an arms agreement with the Soviet Union, President Carter met Soviet President Brezhnev in Vienna and after a series of meetings both men signed SALT II. The President upon his return to the U.S. found a very unhappy Senate opposed to ratifying SALT II arguing that the agreement would put the Russians at an advantage over the United States. The debate between the President and the Senate became academic when the Soviets invaded Afghanistan to put down a rebellion that broke out against the Pro-Soviet government there. President Carter then warned the USSR that any attempt by the Russians to move on the Persian Gulf would mean war with the United States.

Trouble with Iran started when the Shah was overthrown by right-wing Islamic fundamentalists who argued that the Shah was corrupt both in material and spiritual considerations. When the Shah fled the country their religious leader the Ayatollah Khomeini assumed power.

In 1979, President Carter permitted the Shah to enter the U.S. for medical treatment. Following the refusal of the United States to return the Shah to Iran to face trial, the U.S. embassy in Tehran was stormed resulting in the taking of more than fifty American hostages. The militant Iranians refused to release the hostages until the Shah was returned to Iran.

Throughout 1980 Americans were preoccupied with the plight of the Americans held hostage. For over a year the hostage issue was to become the top story in the newspapers and dominated the TV news coverage. An attempt had been made on April 24, 1980 to rescue the hostages but ended in failure when mechanical difficulties forced its postponement, and in disaster when an American helicopter crashed with a transport plane resulting in the death of eight Americans.

The Shah died in 1980 but this was to have no bearing on the American hostages being held in Iran. The war between Iran and Iraq, which started the same year, did not alter the situation either.

President Carter was blamed by many Americans for not taking more aggressive action to secure the release of the hostages. There were those who argued that America should have thrown all of its might to secure their release. The primary concern of President Carter was to see the return of these Americans safe and unharmed and there seemed little else he could do but wait and negotiate for their safe return which he continued to do throughout his last days in office.

With the election of 1980 approaching things did not look very favorable for the reelection bid of the President: the trouble with Iran drove oil prices from $13.00 a barrel in 1978 to over $31.00 a barrel in 1980; inflation was becoming a very real concern to the breadwinners of America; interest rates on loans rose drastically making it difficult for many Americans to

John L. McCloskey

purchase cars and homes and unemployment in America rose from 5.8% in 1979 to 7.1% in 1980. Black Americans' unemployment figures topped 13%.

Popularity polls showed that President Carter was to experience a difficult time in his try for reelection. Some Democrats acutely aware of the uphill battle facing their party in 1980 convinced Senator Edward Kennedy to seek the nomination. President Carter nonetheless had little difficulty receiving the nomination.

The moderate and conservative Republicans patched up the differences that divided them in 1976 and joined forces to stand behind Ronald Reagan as their Presidential candidate. George Bush of Texas was to become Reagan's running mate. John Anderson of Illinois chose not to support Reagan and ran as an independent for the Presidency.

The big issue in the 1980 election was the hostage situation. There wasn't a single issue that touched the hearts of America than those fifty-two U.S. citizens being held captive in Iran and the Republicans used it to their advantage. The shape of the economy was also raised by the Republicans who cast grave doubts over Carter's ability to create a sound economic program.

President Carter let others do the campaigning for him while he remained in Washington working on the hostage situation.

In a series of television debates held between Reagan and Carter critics of Reagan felt it to be paradoxical that he promised to lower the cost of government while at the same time increase defense spending. It seemed to many that Carter was outclassed

126

by the "great communicator" in the debate and the election result seemed to confirm that feeling.

Although polls indicated that the election would be a close one the voters proved them wrong on election day. Reagan polled 489 in the electoral college as opposed to 49 for Carter. The Republicans gained control of the Senate for the first time since 1954 and while still a minority in the House, they increased their numbers.

It was a humiliating defeat for James Earl Carter who worked so hard in the interest of America but had unfortunately fallen victim to the hostage situation which demanded restraint from a country whose inhabitants demanded a quick solution. Jimmy Carter was later to write, "I hope history will deal kindly with me. But I am at peace with the knowledge I did the best I could."

It was just minutes after Ronald Reagan took the oath of office as the fortieth President of the United States that word was received of the release of the fifty-two American hostages. This action proved to be the last spiteful act toward former President Carter who had worked so feverishly to gain their release prior to his leaving office. Their return to American soil was met with wild celebration and very appropriately Jimmy Carter played a major role in the reception.

There were many Americans who had more than a slight suspicion that Reagan had urged the government of Iran to hold up the release of the hostages until after the election of 1980. It seemed, however, to become a moot issue now that "that damned cowboy" was in the White House.

Upon entering office in 1981 Reagan embarked on a program of economics for the nation which has been labeled "Reaganomics", the "Trickle Down" policy and earlier referred to by Bush as "Voodoo economics" during the primary contest he had with Reagan for the Republican nomination in 1980.

Reagan aborted the economic theory practiced since the 1930's which saw the government initiate programs designed to put people to work and thereby enable the citizens to "demand" more services and goods. In its place "Reaganomics" fostered "supply side economics" which he stated would lower taxes on big business resulting in the expansion of business with the desired expectation that unemployment would decline and with more people employed, the economy would improve. It seems that John Adams was accurate when he said that his party, the federalists, an ancestor of the present day Republican Party, "is a party of the rich, able, and well born."

President Reagan, in an attempt to explain the huge national debt incurred during his tenure blamed the "big spenders" in Congress, arguing that he couldn't spend one penny without the consent of Congress.

George Will, a friend of Reagan's and a popular ultra conservative syndicated columnist, countered Reagan's finger pointing by citing that many of the budgets submitted by the administration to Congress totaled over a trillion dollars and that Reagan had proposed 81% of that total.

During Reagan's watch the U.S. went from the greatest creditor nation to the greatest debtor nation. The national debt of $908.5 billion in September, 1980, months prior to Reagan's election, rose to over $2.5 trillion by the time he left office.

The trade deficit reflected that the U.S. was buying considerably more from foreign markets than foreign markets were buying from the U.S. This trade deficit (unfavorable balance of trade) was to become four times as great during Reagan's years in office.

During Reagan's first term, the nation suffered a major recession, the worst since the great crash of 1929. (As a result of the recession, fortunes were lost overnight by millions of investors.) Republicans blamed the tight money policy of the Federal Reserve for soaring interest rates.

President Reagan was faced with great criticism from minority groups who felt that they were being neglected. To keep the noise down, Reagan appointed a woman, Sandra Day O'Connor, to the Supreme Court. This movement did little, however, to allay the harm done to those who had to subsist with fewer government social programs. Cuts in these programs reflected fewer food stamps, public service jobs, student loans, legal services, child nutrition programs, housing subsidies, less Medicare, unemployment compensation, and aid to families with dependent children, a major welfare program.

The attack on the life of President Reagan on March 30, 1981, was not the act of a person suffering from Reagan's social program cutbacks, nor those opposed to his policy of favoring big business, nor the big military spending which met with great opposition, but rather by a young man by the name Hinckley who wanted to impress a young lady actress by the name of Jody Foster.

Hinckley was deemed not to be responsible for his action because of his mental state and so he was institutionalized in a mental facility rather than being incarcerated in prison.

Also injured in the shooting was Reagan's press secretary, Jim Brady. A bill later passed to restrict the sale of hand guns was appropriately called "The Brady Bill", a bill vigorously opposed by the National Rifle Association (NRA) who argued that by taking away law abiding citizens' right to purchase hand guns leaves only the bad guys with the guns.

President Reagan had, earlier in his life, been a Democrat and a fond supporter of FDR's New Deal programs. It seems that as President he stole a page from the New Deal when he created P.I.K. (Payment-In-Kind) which paid the farmers for surplus goods; and also created the Food Security Act, which accounted for direct payments to farmers who limited production, which sounds a lot like Reagan reincarnated the Agriculture Adjustment Act (AAA) of 1936.

The President was not New Dealish in dealing with organized labor. The air traffic controllers made demands that were not honored. Federal law prohibited the group from going on strike and were warned that if they did resort to a strike they would be replaced.

Whether the controllers doubted that the President would replace them and jeopardize air space of if they felt that their cause would not permit them to back down, they decided to call the strike. When this occurred the President fired them all and replaced them with substitutes.

This action brought out the vindictive side of the President, similar to the occasions when he would dare Congress to pass a law objectionable to him with the warning "make my day" ala Clint Eastwood and his Gunsmoke days as an actor.

With the election of 1984 approaching Reagan's campaign group attempted to ferret out a program that would reflect Reagan in a favorable light—they found none. One advantage Reagan possessed for the upcoming election was that the economy had improved from the early days of his presidency. On the negative side was the death of 241 servicemen sent to Beirut by the President one year prior to the election.

A Gallup Poll revealed that during his first two years as President, Reagan had a lower job rating that any President since World War II, including President Carter. This poll would have been detrimental to most incumbent Presidents, but Reagan was no ordinary candidate. With his great communication skills he electrified the electorate and with that inimitable twinkle of his eyes buried his Presidential deficiencies.

The Democrats had chosen Walter Mondale as their choice for the Presidency and Geraldine Ferraro, the first woman to run for V.P., as his running mate.

The Democrats were well aware of the uphill battle they were to experience in expelling popular Reagan, but they felt that there were enough deficiencies in his tenure to bring about a major upset, particularly the social program cuts.

Reagan injected a bit of humor to the campaign when, during the debate with Mondale, he was asked it he thought at age 73 he wasn't too old for the job. Reagan replied that he was not going to make age an issue in the campaign. "I am not going to exploit, for political purposes, my opponent's youth and inexperience."

The results of the election trumpeted a resounding victory for the President. Reagan carried 49 states. Mondale carried only Minnesota and the District of Columbia.

In foreign affairs, President Reagan was obsessed with destroying Communism wherever it occurred. His chief target was the Soviet Union, which was diametrically opposed to any attempt of the U.S. to curb Communism, and so the cold war continued between the two world powers. Reagan once referred to the Soviet Union as an evil empire in a major speech he delivered.

Fearful that troubles which broke out in Central America, and particularly Nicaragua, would jeopardize U.S. security, the President interceded in the troubles between the Sandinista regime and the Contras.

The President and his advisors decided to aid the Contras in any way they could. Congress, on the other hand, did not share the feeling of the administration and decided to withhold any funds intended for that purpose.

The CIA with the alleged knowledge and support of the administration, chose alternative ways to aid the Contras. They made a deal with Saudi Arabia whereby the Saudis would provide financial assistance to the

Contras in exchange for the U.S. providing them with missiles needed by the Saudis to protect their oil tankers. This exchange was consummated when, with Congress out of town, the President invoked an emergency rule and secretly flew four hardened missiles to Saudi Arabia without waiting for the approval of Congress.

When the press started to question the quest of money from foreign governments to support the Contras, the House Intelligence Committee summoned CIA Director, Casey, for an explanation. When asked by the committee if any other country was approached by the U.S. to give aid to the Contras, the Director replied, "not to my knowledge"—a direct lie.

To stem the tide of the activity in the Reagan administration of circumventing the ruling of Congress, the Boland Amendment was passed by Congress, prohibiting the CIA or "any other agency or entity involved in intelligence activities" from spending money directly or indirectly to support the rebels.

Oliver North who had been put in charge of the operation boldly stated that the White House wasn't covered by the amendment. At one point, it was reported that North held up a copy of the Boland Amendment and stated, "This is the law I'm breaking every day," a statement he denied ever having made.

In the Middle East disputes developed between the Christians and the Moslems in Lebanon. The Lebanese government had the support of Russia-backed Syria and this posed concern on the part of the U.S.

President Reagan, in an effort to resolve the difficulties between the Muslims and Christians and hopefully to end the marriage between Lebanon and Syria dispatched U.S. Marines to Lebanon.

When the Marines' role turned to that of helping the Lebanese government which was controlled by the Christians, it incurred the wrath of the Muslim faction. The U.S. became convinced that it was merely a matter of time before a Syrian takeover of Lebanon following the Muslim shelling of the Lebanese government forces.

Following the shelling by the Muslims the U.S. became an active player in the Lebanese Civil War. The big guns of the U.S.S. New Jersey, which had been sent to the area, shelled Muslim Villages. In retaliation for this shelling a Muslim suicide bomber rammed a truck full of explosives into the center of the main Marine barracks at the Beirut Airport killing 241 American servicemen.

When the radical Muslim forces took over half of Beirut the U.S. forces were sent to the fleet offshore to insure their safe departure.

This incident in the Middle East is but one example of Reagan's bungling of foreign affairs. He gave no direction to his staff but rather let them decide the best course to take. This accounts to a large extent for the Secretaries of State and Defense to be at odds as to what the President really wanted.

Whenever the President met with foreign dignitaries, he was supplied with 3 x 5 cards with pertinent information on them. Alexander Haig, Reagan's first Secretary of State, urged the President to set aside just one hour a week to study foreign issues. There was no evidence that this was ever done.

During the summer of 1985 word was received by President Reagan that TWA Flight 847, which had landed in Beirut, had been hijacked by Muslim gunmen. Thirty-nine American passengers and crew were being held hostage. The demands of the Muslims called for the release of 700 Lebanese prisoners being held in Israeli jails and it would be the job of the U.S. government to convince the Israelis to meet that demand. To show that they meant business, the hijackers cold bloodedly killed a young Navy diver by shooting him in the head and dumping his body out of the plane in plain view of all to see.

The worm had turned for President Reagan. He took full credit in 1981 for the release of the hostages being held during the Carter administration, and vowed that any future incidents like that would be met with force; we would never yield to demands from terrorist groups. Those statements would come back to haunt the President.

It was somewhat paradoxical that the United States would urge other countries of the world not to sell arms to Iran when, in fact, this is precisely what the U.S. did when they authorized an Israeli shipment of arms to Iran in exchange for the release of the hostages. Altogether there were five such deals negotiated with Iran the last of which "coincidentally" was timed just prior to the election of 1986.

When news of the hostage deals became public, the Reagan administration popularity hit a new low and the U.S. was disgraced on the world scene for its hypocrisy. In the U.S. the Tower Board was set up to investigate the incidents. President Reagan was summoned to determine what role, if any, he played in the arms for hostages deals. Reagan had been prepared by his advisors on how to handle the questions to be asked of him—he simply could not remember. Satisfied that the President had been adequately prepped they relaxed. However, when asked by the board whether he had authorized the Israeli shipment of arms to Iran his answer was "yes", completely shocking the White House aides who had prepped him for the questioning.

Once again, Reagan was called before the Tower Board and was again asked if he had authorized the August arms shipment in advance. This time he read the answer that aides had prepared for him that he was completely surprised upon learning of the Israeli arms shipment. He also continued to read the instructions the aides had written for him. The investigators were left numb.

When new revelations became public that were extremely damaging for the Reagan administration, a key player in the administration, Bud McFarland, attempted suicide. In the meantime, another key player, Oliver North, was earning the title "Prince of Shredders" while he and his secretary vigorously fed the shredding machine with information damaging to the administration.

At the insistence of his aides, the President called a press conference to clean up the "misunderstanding". Always before, the Great Communicator was able to convince the public with his charm but this was not to be this time. The popularity polls suggested that he really didn't belong in that high office; the polls would confirm what his top advisors had felt for years.

Several years after Reagan left office it was revealed that the President was suffering from Alzheimer's Disease. This revelation was to answer a lot of questions that plagued many people for years—perhaps he really couldn't remember.

As the election of 1988 approached, a poll taken that year revealed that the public wanted the next President to "get the nation on a new direction," not to "keep the country moving in the direction that Ronald Reagan had been taking"—an obvious sign of displeasure with the Reagan years.

The Republicans chose George Bush Vice president during the Reagan years, as their standard-bearer. On the ticket with Bush was Dan Quayle, Senator from Indiana.

Michael Dukakis, Governor of Massachusetts, was nominated by the Democratic Party, and with him on the ticket was Lloyd Benson, Senator from Texas.

During the campaigning a cloud hung over the head of Bush over his role in the arms for hostages deals. He argued that he was "out of the loop", but there was rather convincing evidence that Bush was mired in the thick of the arms for hostages deals. Like Reagan, Bush denied any knowledge of the affair although the minutes of a meeting in which Bush was President showed that he had been briefed in detail of the deals. Also, like Reagan, he referred to Oliver North as a "hero".

Dukakis was attacked by the Republicans for the conditions at Boston Harbor, a slap at his environmental concerns, and also for being soft on crime.

To strengthen their charge of being soft on crime, the Republicans cited the case of Willie Horton, a black prisoner whose sentence was commuted by Governor Dukakis, and later was to be involved in a brutal murder. There is little doubt that the Willy Horton incident became the "ace in the hole" for the Republicans.

A series of debates were held in which the major issues of the country were discussed—crime, drugs, unemployment, foreign affairs concerns. It was during one of the debates between the Vice Presidential candidate, Benson, and Quayle that Quayle invoked the name of John F. Kennedy. At that point Benson turned to Quayle and said, "I worked with President Kennedy. He was my friend. Senator, you are no John F. Kennedy." When Quayle expressed annoyance with Benson's remark Benson replied, "You're the one who made the comparison, Senator." (There were many who felt that Benson would have been a more formidable opponent of Bush since Benson had defeated Bush previously for the Senate seat of Texas.)

The election results were a victory for Bush and Quayle. Bush had promised a "kinder, gentler nation" if elected.

It is difficult to determine whether the voters wanted a stronger, gentler nation, or whether they were reluctant to support a virtual unknown on the national scene. Bush was no stranger to politics, having served for eight years as Vice President under Ronny and Nancy.

Following Bush's victory the subject of taxation arose. Bush asserted that there would be no new taxes. "Read my lips—no new taxes," was a promise he made which was later to haunt him following his signature to a new tax law. To many, Bush showed a weak side by reneging on his promise. It tore his party apart and likely hurt many Republican candidates in the mid-term election of 1990.

Bush's domestic program—many questioned if there was one—was anemic at best. Bush felt that status quo would be the way to go.

Time Magazine portrayed Bush as a success in foreign affairs and a failure in handling domestic issues.

In the Persian Gulf, however, a serious problem arose when Iraq invaded Kuwait. Following the mid-term elections, Bush announced a resolution to take action against Iraq and Saddam Hussein in an effort to free Kuwait.

The Gulf War in which the U.S. engaged was a major victory for the U.S. but fell short of ridding Saddam Hussein who, for many years, would be a threat to the nations of the Middle East. It was later learned that many of the objectives of the war were never achieved—success of bombing missions was grossly exaggerated—but it was enough to satisfy the insatiable appetite of Americans for victory, Americans who still felt the pains of defeat from the Vietnam War.

Parades were held throughout the United States. The sale of American flags swelled and those proud veterans who were fortunate enough to survive the war held their heads high. The stock of President Bush rose to new heights and it became clear to the Democrats that the confidence they had of unseating Bush prior to the Gulf War was dashed.

The euphoria immediately following the Gulf War somehow would not last. There were domestic issues to be addressed. Bush's domestic program had not improved and the American public while recognizing a favorable foreign policy, could not excuse him for the lack of leadership on domestic issues and his reneging on his promise of no new taxes.

As the election of 1992 approached, the Democrats nominated Bill Clinton, governor of Arkansas, as their standard bearer. Al Gore, Senator from Tennessee, was to be his running mate.

His reputation as an adulterer was well promulgated by those opposed to his nomination, but to many his views echoed a solid program.

The Gennifer Flowers affair was certain to be brought up during the campaign followed by scores of other charges of infidelity. These charges prompted the Clinton group to keep a file on the investigation of these charges and called it the "Doomsday Files" in preparation to answer charges when they arose. The Doomsday Files covered allegations of Bush's affairs. They felt that these files would prevent Bush from using infidelity as an issue in the campaign.

The charges of infidelity would not stand in the way of Clinton's victories in 1992 and again in 1996, but they were far from being forgotten.

Other charges were also brought up including Clinton's demonstrations against the Vietnam War while a Rhodes Scholar in England. This charge did not sit well with Vietnam's groups and other star spangled Americans.

He also was charged with being a pot smoker, and when asked if he ever smoked pot, he admitted that he tried it but didn't inhale. This statement gave a lot of material for the late night show hosts and stand-up comics, as one might expect.

Clinton's choice of Gore from the neighboring state of Tennessee to share the ticket with him led many to question whether Gore was a wise choice since he came from the neighboring state of Clinton's Arkansas. It was felt that a running mate from another section of the nation might produce more votes, but Clinton liked Gore and it was his call.

President Bush became the obvious candidate of the Republican Party and again chose Dan Quayle as his running mate despite a feeling by many that Quayle would hurt Bush's chance of winning the election.

Ross Perot didn't care much for the stand taken by the Republicans and Democrats and organized a third party. He was a Texas billionaire who, with chart after chart, showed the American people how he would solve the financial troubles facing the nation. He was to acquire a following that alarmed the Democrats since they felt that Perot would hurt them more than hurt the Republicans. Perot did win the first debate and this caused the Democrats to "roll up their sleeves."

The election results gave Clinton the victory but with only 43 per cent of the vote making him a minority President.

Ross Perot gained 19 per cent of the vote and this signaled a need for Clinton to "flirt" (he was good at that) with the attractive planks of the Perot platform, particularly the budget deficit which had been the main thrust of the Perot program.

Early in the Clinton administration troubled developed: the appointment of Zoë Baird for the Whitehouse Counsel job was jeopardized when it was learned that she had hired illegal immigrants. Clinton was to admit he erred in rushing through his cabinet appointments; by lifting restrictions placed previously on abortions incurring the wrath of pro-life supporters; by proposing to end the ban on homosexuals in the military which raised the fur of the military and military service organizations.

A major thrust of Clinton's program was to end welfare "as we know it." He wanted to put people off the welfare rolls and back to work; he achieved some success with his program.

Clinton also attempted to alter the health care system so as to make medical care available to all. He appointed his wife, Hillary, to head the program. The program presented by Hillary met with serious opposition from across the aisle and so it was never implemented.

President Clinton worked feverishly to come up with a method for reducing the Federal deficit. He finally, with his advisors, came up with a complex program aimed at balancing the national budget and reducing the national debt which he later was able to accomplish during his second term.

On foreign affairs Clinton had sort of an anemic interest. He had inherited many of the troubles of Europe and the Middle East and wished that they would go away and permit him to get back to solving the social problems facing the nations. This was not to be. The civil war in Bosnia among the Muslims, Serbs, and Croats had to be addressed. The President knew that in order for the U.S. to continue to be the world leader, some action would have to be taken.

An early plan of the President to resolve the problems in Bosnia was a program called "lift and strike" which didn't fly with other countries so the idea was abandoned.

The shelling of Sarajevo by the Bosnian Serbs, however, heightened the need for some kind of action and with the feeling that there was adequate support among our allies. The matter was taken before NATO. The air strikes suggested and encouraged by the President, never materialized to a great extent because the Secretary-General of the U.N., Boutros Boutros-Ghali, declared that only he had the authority to call for NATO intervention in Bosnia.

Ultimately, the choice of the President was to increase the humanitarian aid to Bosnia—a poor substitute for ground troops—angered those in favor of U.S. military action. Military action, the only choice we had, angered others.

As the mid-term elections of November, 1994 neared, there was much concern that Clinton would lose members of his party. The problem of his draft-dodging, pot smoking charges gave way to charged that he and his wife, Hillary, engaged in illegal political and financial dealings while he was governor of Arkansas, which became known as the Whitewater affair. Also the charges that Clinton had state troopers escort woman to the governor's mansion and to the back seat of police cars raised a few eyebrows—just a few.

The election of 1996 was approaching so it became necessary for the political parties to have their infamous conventions. It was a foregone conclusion that the Democratic incumbent would be the choice of the Democratic convention. Once again, Al Gore was chosen as his running mate. The Republicans chose Bob Dole, former majority leader of the Senate (he resigned to run for President) and, as his running mate he chose Jack Kemp. Senator from New York. Dole and Kempt had patched up their earlier differences to form a united team.

During the campaign Dole hoped that his service in the military, which left him disabled, would help sway the voters; his running mate, Kemp, also had a distinguished career in the military. Dole's age was to become a factor in this election. Also his straight-laced countenance was in direct contrast to President Clinton's personality.

Clinton was felt by many to be vulnerable in light of the recent charges leveled against him in the

Whitewater scandal and charges of sexual improprieties.

The President won a second term but any satisfaction enjoyed by the Democrats was soon to dissolve in light of charges leveled against the President by Paula Jones who, as a worker in the Democratic camp accused the President of sexual misconduct when he was Governor of Arkansas.

During the heated Whitewater charges, the Attorney General of the U.S., Janet Reno, appointed Kenneth Starr as a special prosecutor to investigate the charges. Unable to find anything illegal about Clinton's activities in the case, he then asked for and received permission from the Attorney General to focus on the sexual misconduct of the President.

Eventually the Paula Jones case was dismissed by Judge Susan Webber Wright, but a shocking revelation occurred when a young intern at the White House, Monica Lewinsky, confided to her friend, Linda Tripp, that she had engaged in sex with the president many times while visiting the White House. Linda Tripp recorded these conversations with Monica Lewinsky and promptly turned them over to Kenneth Starr. Starr then outfitted Linda Tripp with an FBI body wire to gather more incriminating information.

Nothing became more boring to the people of the U.S. than Starr's investigation of the President; Starr could possibly have surpassed Linda Tripp as the most hated in America. Many polls were eventually taken to determine the attitude of the American people toward the investigation. Poll after poll showed that the public felt that the President should be judged on his programs and not on his personal life. The thought of resignation, which the conservative Republicans and some Democrats were calling for, was never well received by the President. It seems that the expression, "It's the economy, stupid!" was never truer than at this period in our history.

In a desperate attempt to "nail down" the President, Kenneth Starr granted immunity from prosecution to Monica Lewinsky if she were to come forth with information that would dispute Clinton's testimony. She accepted the offer and, in new testimony, acknowledged that she and the President had had an affair.

In light of this admission by Lewinsky, the President was urged by his advisors to come forth and confess that he had betrayed his family and the nation. His admission came short of saying that he lied when he denied having sexual relations with "that woman." This failure to admit that he lied did not sit well with his critics who continued to push for impeachment of the President. With the admission by the President that he had misled the American people in the Monica Lewinsky charges, the Paula Jones case was then put back on the front burner, ending with the President paying $850,000 to Paula Jones to settle the case.

While Clinton's fate was being decided, once again trouble developed with Iraq when Saddam Hussein refused to permit the U.N. inspection team to hunt out weapons of mass destruction.

A great force of Naval weapons and land forces was dispatched to the Persian Gulf and despite threats from Russia that any action taken by the U.S. against

Iraq would result in strained relations with the two countries and possibly lead to Word War III, it did not halt U.S. buildup in the Gulf.

Many people suspected that the action taken by the U.S. was an attempt by the President to take the "heat" off him at home. This suspicion did not deter the President from ordering daily air strikes at the missile sites of Iraq.

When Kenneth Starr completed his investigation, he then submitted the data to the House Judiciary Committee to determine whether charges should be brought for potential impeachment. When the Judiciary Committee felt there was sufficient cause to impeach the President, the full House then concurred with the committee and, voting along strict party lines, decided to send the case to the U.S. Senate for trial.

To most Americans there was no question that the conservative Republicans were bent on "getting" Clinton at all costs. This vendetta likely could have been an attempt to get a "level playing field" in light of the fact that both President Nixon and Vice President Agnew had resigned in disgrace, and were probably still smarting over the Iran-Contra investigation.

By this time many Republican Congressmen, up for reelection in 1998, worried that the Party may have shot itself in the foot by prolonging an investigation that had become so distasteful to the American Public. They were right, in an off year election the Party not represented in the White House generally increases their representation; the Republicans actually lost membership to their Democratic opponents.

John L. McCloskey

During the Senate impeachment trial of President Clinton, several plans were proposed for resolving the situation: present a motion to dismiss the charges; have a formal censure of the President; continue on with the trial to the bitter end.

The Senate, mindful of the attitude of the American voters to bring an end to the situation, pressed on for an early solution. Their promise of handling the case in a bipartisan manner met with some success, and in the final balloting, the President was found to be not guilty of the perjury charges and also the obstruction of justice charge.

The second impeachment of a President of the U.S. was now put to rest. How history will treat the Clinton impeachment remains to be seen but it seems that there is general agreement that the charges of sexual misconduct, perjury under oath, and obstruction of justice while admittedly showing low moral standards by the President and incurring disgrace for the U.S. Presidency did not constitute removal from office since it didn't meet the criteria of high crimes and misdemeanors as intended by our founding fathers.

Notes

1. "Waving the bloody shirt" was a strategy employed by the Republicans to remind the voters that the Democratic party was the perpetrator of the War Between the States.

2. The Republican party shed the Union label following the war.

3. The Stalwarts were furious when Hayes dismissed Chester A. Arthur as the Collector of the Port of New York for misconduct in office. New York, after all, was Conkling's turf and Arthur was a Stalwart.

4. Gresham's Law: Bad money will drive good money out of circulation.

ABOUT THE AUTHOR

John McCloskey is a retired teacher of U.S. history. For twelve years he taught in the Coatesville, PA School District, and twenty-two years at Brandywine High School, Wilmington, DE, a part of the early Alfred I. du Pont School District and now part of the Brandywine School District.

His educational background consists of a B.S. from The University of Scranton, a masters degree from The University of Delaware and a masters plus thirty with an administrative certificate from The University of Delaware.

Mr. McCloskey and his wife, Marie, reside in Wilmington, DE, and are the parents of seven children, grandparents of sixteen and great-grandparents of one.

www.ingramcontent.com/pod-product-compliance
Lightning Source LLC
Chambersburg PA
CBHW020431290526
45785CB00002B/803